KAIVALYADHAMA

LONAVLA

KAIVALYADHAMA

YOGA FOR THE WORLD

KAIVALYADHAMA

YOGA FOR THE WORLD

TEACHING METHODS FOR YOGIC PRACTICES

By
Dr. M.L. Gharote
and
Dr. S.K. Ganguly

KAIVALYADHAMA
Swami Kuvalayananda Marg,
Lonavla - 410 403, INDIA

KAIVALYADHAMA
Swami Kuvalayananda Marg,
Lonavla - 410 403, INDIA
Kaivalyadhama Samiti, Lonavla.

First Published 1988
Second Published 2001
Third Publised January 2011
Fourth Published April 2017
Fifth Published April 2018
Sixth Published March 2019
Seventh Published 26 Jan 2023

This book received the first Prize at the 20th & 21st National Prize Competition for published Literature on Physical Education, Sports Sciences and Yoga Related to physical Education etc. in the year 1989-90

ISBN : 97-88189485-24-5

Rs : 350/-

Printed in India

At Unique Offset 50/7/A Narhe Gaon, Dhayari Narhe Road Pune - 411 041 and Published by **Kaivalyadhama S.M.Y.M. Samiti,** Lonavla, Dist. Pune 410403

DEDICATION

This book is dedicated to the sacred memory of Swami Kuvalayananda, the founder of Kaivalyadhama, a great personality, who could foresee the immense scope for the application of Yoga in all the spheres of life. It was mainly his scientific technique of teaching, which led the world towards a new direction in the field of Yoga Science.

M. L. Gharote
S. K. Ganguly

Foreword

Swami Shivanandaji of Rishikesh (Uttaranchala) and Swami Kuvalayanandaji of Kaivalyadhama, Lonavla (Maharashtra), were two great names in the history of Yoga, especially, its systematic training to aspirants. The former started the Yoga-Vedanta Forest University, and the latter, the very first College of Yoga and Cultural Synthesis. Both these pioneers started their work in the first half of the twentieth century, and with slow but steady progress, that work of systematic training in Yoga has now spread considerably in many parts of the world. Now, in the beginning of the twentyfirst century, many individuals and institutions are found to engage themselves in teaching Yoga by taking Yoga classes and by treating patients through yogic methods. These people are usually drawn from the basic disciplines of Physical Education, Ayurveda, or even modern medicine. By and large, they themselves are not very proficient in teaching methodology. They seem to look upon Yoga training as a profession or a performing art like, for example, photography, painting or carpentry. There is no harm in having this tendency, if one has honesty and devotion. But it is imperative that every Yoga teacher must be aware of the importance of knowing the teaching methods and principles well and their application to Yoga. For that purpose, this would be a very useful book. One's performance as a Yoga teacher would be improved by studying this book.

Pune - 25th June 2001

Kalidas Joshi
Ex-Head of the Department
of Yogic, Studies,
Hari Singh Sagar University,
Sagar (M.P.)

PREFACE - I

The teaching of yogic practices is a new experience for students, teachers and beginning teachers alike. This book is intended to serve as a guide to lead from the unknown territory of teaching Yoga to the known territory of successful and efficient teaching of yogic practices. It is hoped that it will smoothen the path of the student-teacher or a new teacher of Yoga and afford a happier and more profitable learning experience on the part of the Yoga students.

Before one begins teaching Yoga it is necessary that the teacher is fully convinced about the contributions that various practices can make in the area of Education and for the well being of children and young people as well as adult students. The teacher should be fully aware of the unique benefits of the programme of yogic practices to the growth and development of individual students in relation to the other school programmes. Without realising these preliminaries to teaching, the teacher will not be able to make available the rich and rewarding experiences of yogic practices to the participants. The teaching of a class must result in a happy and pleasant experience.

"Teaching Methodology of Yogic Practices" has been a curriculum subject for the students of the G.S.College of Yoga and Cultural Synthesis for many years. It is also becoming an essential subject in the training courses of Yoga teachers elsewhere. The authors have been long associated with the handling of this subject in the G.S. College of Yoga and Cultural Synthesis and this book is based on their personal experience of teaching students at many different levels of development.

We feel that there is such a dearth of literature on this subject that both experienced Yoga teachers and beginning teachers will derive benefits in their field from this book.

Although we have been contemplating in bringing out this book for some time, it has only now become possible due to financial help from the Ministry of Human Resources Development, Govt. of India, New Delhi for which we are grateful.

- M. L. Gharote
- S. K. Ganguly

PREFACE - II

Teaching is a specialised subject. In all teaching learning situation, it is very essential that a student as well as the teacher should know the techniques and art of teaching. There is no exception to yogic teaching also. More so, when one goes to teach Yoga practices, one should have a hand book like this as ready made material. Till date there was no teaching methodology book, except this, available in the field of Yoga practices. Therefore, it was necessary to publish this book which can guide students as well as the would be teachers in the field of Yoga.

The first edition of this book is almost sold as it has got a demand in different colleges and universities where Yoga is being taught. Looking to the need of the day, this book has been edited so far mistakes are concerned and also a new material in the form of **Index** has been added to it. This will further facilitate the readers in locating immediately the topic that he wants to go through. This was then left earlier due to short of time. Moreover, the book has been given a new shape to look at.

Since it is a curriculum subject in Gordhandas Seksaria College of Yoga and Cultural Synthesis, it is hoped that students will get maximum benefit while going through this as a guide book.

- M.L.Gharote

-S.K.Ganguly

PREFACE-III

Tradition of teaching has a long history of thousand years in India. The "Gurukulas" established by Rishis and Munis were abode of learning. It is a noble job and ideal profession but it requires a skill on the part of the teacher. No doubt teachers are born and not made, but certain skill and good methodology can change the whole teaching in a class room situation. Therefore, it is our effort to bring about a book on "Teaching methods for Yoga practices" for it has come into the realm of education. The role of a teacher is not merely teaching but effective teaching so that the students learn the lesson effectively. This new edition has got two important chapters added to it. One is utility of teaching aids with little addition into it and the second one is "How to put questions in a classroom situation" to test the merit of the sadhaka (learner). Moreover, at the end, some selected "Model questions" are added to this edition from examination point of view for it is an examination subject in the Gordhandas Seksaria College of Yoga & Cultural Synthesis. The author believes that the Yoga teachers as well as the students will be benefited to understand and apply such points further for better presentation of the subject matter. It has also replaced its earlier black and white photographs for progressive way of teaching the selected yogic practices. In this context, helps were taken from Ms. Suchint Kaur Sodhi, Yoga Instructor and Miss.Surabhi Rattan, Shri Suman Dutta and Sri Ankan Kumar Sarkar our students. My thanks go to each of these people. I am indebted to Rev. Swami Maheshanandaji, Chairman and to Sri O. P. Tiwariji, Secretary, K. S. M. Y. M. Samiti for constant guidance and encouragement for the improvement of this book.

I end my preface with Swami Kuvalayanandaji's saying based on his comment on Teacher in education. He said, "A teacher should have a motherly love for his students. One cannot win over students either through creating a personal awe and fear or through creating an aura of one's knowledge and scholarly panache. Teachers should never insult and should never use abrasive words to such students in any ways. Such students should be treated more affectionately and should be encouraged. Give some more time to such students even after the usual school hours. A teacher perceives, instantly, through bodily cues as to whether a particular students has understood the subject matter. He should see to it that the subject matter being taught is thoroughly understood by such a student.

Every teacher should cognize his responsibility for value education and physical education along with formal education. Be it any subject, a teacher should emphasize on value inculcation and ethical values while planning out teaching of his subject matter. It would not be pertinent to leave the subject of Physical Education to the respective subject teacher only. As well, this subject should not be treated as merely a part of sports activities. In a class room situation, during a learning process, even the mode of sitting, standing and conducting oneself properly, can be encompassed within the ambit of physical education. From the view point of biological science all these aspects of human endeavors have an intimate relationship with health and hygiene. With due cognizance to this fact, the class teacher concerned should guide students appropriately. A teacher will be able to perform his above mentioned duties only when he has a motherly love for his students".

- S. K. Ganguly

Preface IV

The teaching methodology is almost paramount factor in any teacher' Training center. Yoga is not exception to that. It has got a demand in different colleges and universities in India where yoga is being taught. In this new publication, one more new chapter has been added with by the name "Guideline to organize Nonresidential Yoga camp". This will further facilitate the yoga teachers to handle the yoga classes in a camp. Today, teaching is a time bound work. Not everything can be taught in a residential school or college. Neither every individual can effort to come to learn nor every individual who so ever wishes to learn yoga practices can be admitted in the yoga course. Therefore, there is a need to organize the yoga teaching in different cities also where they can can come and get the similar advantages of it in the yoga camp. Lastly, I am indebted to Dr. O.P.Tiwariji, Chairman, Kaivalyadhama for going through this manuscript critically. I am also extremely thankful to Prof. R.K. Bodheji as well as to Dr. Bandita Satpathi, Principal of the college to give some feedback in the above article.

Dr. S.K. Ganguly

CONTENTS

INTRODUCTION

Chapter 1

INTRODUCTION

We have very little information about the ways and methods resorted to by the teachers in ancient times for teaching various subjects. However, according to Bhagwat Gita the methods of learning consisted of persistent questioning, showing reverence and doing physical work for the teacher. There were no fixed hours of teaching. There were no examinations and no certificates. Being with the teacher was the best way to learn. The relations between the teacher and the students were free and frank. Often there were arguments between the teacher and the student but this never led to any acrimony. Before any lesson began, the teacher and the student would both pray together that they might derive the best results. The idea was to study together, not to compete with each other. The teacher always knew more than the student but he did not claim that he knew everything. A good teacher always expected that his student should prove his superiority. All learning took place in the residential situation. All education was completely free. Most of the teaching was oral, so this required recitation and cultivation of a good memory. The student not only learned from the content of the lessons but through personal conduct, which was expected to be above reproach.

Teaching of a practical subject involved observation, demonstration and practice on the part of the student and correction of the faults, giving positive suggestions by the teacher. There was also much use of the trial and error method on the part of the student.

Teaching was not a profession but a mission to enlighten innocent young children entrusted to the care of teachers.

Most of the teaching was individualised using instructional method on a one-to-one basis or at the most in a small group.

Today the times have changed. Like other professions teaching has also become a profession. However, the teaching of Yoga differs from other forms of teaching. For the first time in history, Yoga has attracted the attention of enormous numbers of people all round the world and we find it necessary to devise different methods of instruction for class work in order to fulfill the needs of so many interested students. Hence we have evolved from our experience some methods of teaching yogic practices to train the maximum number of persons with minimum expenditure of time and effort.

YOGA AND YOGIC PRACTICES

Chapter 2

YOGA AND YOGIC PRACTICES

Yoga is a very ancient discipline. It is recognised as one of the most important and valuable heritages of India. Today, the whole world is looking to Yoga for the answer to various problems modern man is facing. At no time in the past has Yoga attracted so much attention from people in so many places in the world. In spite of this fact, no field is so grossly misunderstood as Yoga, even in India. If we were to take a cross section of society and make a general survey of the public's opinion about Yoga, we would find many mis-conceptions about Yoga, the most common of which are :

i) Yoga is not meant for the ordinary person, the house-holder but is only for a select few.

ii) Yoga is associated with the idea of the supernatural or linked with miracles.

iii) Yoga is equated with mysticism, black magic or various types of mortification.

iv) Yoga is a system of therapy which can cure all diseases.

v) Yoga is a system of philosophy dealing with metaphysical theories about the universe.

vi) Yoga is just a system of exercise.

All these misconceptions indicate that most people are unable to see Yoga as a whole concept, but are only aware of a fragment of its potential.

The term "Yoga" is used in the literature both as an end as well as means. As an end yoga signifies 'integration of personality' at the highest level. One of the meanings of Yoga derived from the root 'yuj' is SAMADHI. It is a comprehensive term really means 'integration' and includes in it all other meanings. Samatva or harmony is another word which suggests the same meaning. This is the meaning of Yoga as an end.

In order to help the development of such integration, various techniques are employed. These techniques or practices are mentioned in the yogic literature and are also referred to collectively as Yoga'. Thus we find various individual practices coupled with the term Yoga like Netiyoga, Laulikiyoga, Dhyanayoga and so on. When various practices are systematized and formed into a discipline employing such practices, these systems are known as 'schools' of Yoga like Bhaktiyoga, J nanayoga, Karmayoga, Hathayoga, Layayoga and so on.

Thus, it will be seen that the word 'Yoga' is traditionally used to convey the meaning of an 'end' as well as a 'means'. Lack of discrimination between these two meanings is one of the causes of confusion about Yoga.

The discipline of Yoga passed through several stages and in the course of time different schools emerged which had evolved a variety of techniques and practices. Every school of Yoga emphasized specific practices, but their aim always remained the same : the highest level of integration through the control of the modifications of mind. Some schools use practices that deal with the mind directly and some use indirect means through the body to tackle mental processes.

All the yogic practices may be classified as (i) Asanas, (ii) Pranayamas, (iii) Bandhas and Mudras, (iv) Kriyas, (v) Meditation and (vii) Attitude training practices. Each one of these classifications consists of a group of several practices. Let us now get acquainted with these groups.

ASANAS:

These are special patterns of postures that stabilise the mind and the body through static stretchings. Their aim is to establish proper rhythm in the neuromuscular tonic impulses and improve the general muscle tone.

The two basic principles governing the performance of Asanas are stability and comfort. This suggests that the nature of Asanas is psychophysical and not only physical. Although they are practised by the body the effect on the mind is also felt.

Every Asana should be performed effortlessly and maintained for a comfortable time. There should be no jerks and the performances of Asanas should not lead to undue fatigue.

Asanas may be classified as (1) Meditative, (2) Cultural and (3) Relaxative.

1) Meditative Asanas are sitting postures which maintain the body in a steady and comfortable condition. By various arrangements of the legs and hands different Meditative Asanas are formed. The characteristics feature of the Meditative Asanas is, however, keeping the head, neck and trunk straight..

2) ***Cultural Asanas*** involve static stretchings which bring about proper tone of the muscles. They contribute to the flexibility of the spine and render back and spinal muscles stronger. They also stimulate proper working of the vital organs in the thoracic and abdominal cavities. There are innumerable varieties of cultural asanas which are performed in sitting, lying and standing positions.

3) ***Relaxative Asanas*** are few in number. They are performed in the lying position and are meant for giving rest to the body and mind.

Asanas in general form the basis of other yogic practices by preparing an adequate background.

PRANAYAMAS:

These practices bring control over the respiratory impulses which form one of the channels of the flow of autonomic nerve impulses. Holding of the breath for a prolonged and comfortable time is an essential technique of Pranayama. However, in the initial practice the breath holding phase is completely avoided and emphasis is put on the controlled inspiration and expiration with a time ratio of 1:2 between them. The expiratory phase is so controlled that the following inspiratory phase is not affected in its slow and controlled inspiration.

There are many varieties of Pranayama which use different permutations and combinations of breathing techniques through one or two nostrils or sometimes inspiration through the mouth.

The three phases of Pranayama, namely controlled inspiration, controlled retention and controlled expiration are technically known as Puraka, Kumbhaka and Rechaka respectively.

The main purpose of Pranayama is to gain control over the autonomic nervous system and through it influence the mental function. It is useful in higher yogic practices like meditation.

BANDHAS AND MUDRAS:

These are locks and holds of the semi-voluntary and involuntary muscles in the body. They decongest the vital organs, improve circulation and nutrition by pressure manipulations and contribute to general health and emotional stability. A difference is made between the Bandhas and Mudras on the basis of their use in Pranayama. Mudras that are used in Pranayama are usually called Bandhas because they bind and channelise a particular nervous activity in a particular place or direction. J alandhara, Uddiyana and Mula are important Bandhas. Some Asanas are called Mudras because of their specific and channels through which the effects are brought about.

KRIYAS:

These are purification processes usually classified into six divisions and therefore they are often called Shatkriyas. These are Dhauti, Basti, Neti, Trataka, Nauli and Kapalabhati, each one of which consist of many subsections. They increase the range of adaptability of the tissues forming various organs and systems and raise the threshold of their reactivity. Kriyas bring control on different reflexes and establish psychophysiological balance. The modes of purification in the kriyas are air, water, friction and manipulating movements. The regions of cleansing involved in various kriyas are Nasopharyngeal, orocranial, gastroaesophageal, anorectal and intestinal.

MEDITATION:

This is the practice involving control of the mental functions which start from the initial withdrawal of the senses from external objects to the complete oblivion of the external environment. There are innumerable techniques of meditation. It is a process of absorption in which the individual tries to turn his attention to dwell upon a single object, sound, concept or experience.

Meditation is a great tranquilliser. However, it is not always safe to start one's practice in Meditation without preparing adequately through Asanas and Pranayama. In the hierarchy of yogic practices Meditation occupies a higher position. The basic principle of Meditation is to develop internal awareness.

ATTITUDE TRAINING PRACTICES:

These are technically called Yamas and Niyamas. These are self imposed restrictions to govern one's behavior to form a particular attitudinal pattern. These form the basis of all the yogic practices.

The nature of all yogic practices is psychophysical. All yogic practices are complementary to each other and each practice contributes to similar effects on a greater or lesser scale using different channels and approaches.

MEANING AND SCOPE OF TEACHING METHODS

Chapter 3

MEANING AND SCOPE OF TEACHING METHODS

Teaching is a part of the educational process which involves the following factors :

1) Teaching - A process involving methods.
2) Learning - A process of adjustment through action.
3) Teacher - A person who directs the process.
4) Student - A person who adjusts himself through the action.
5) Subject of Activity - Content of learning.
6) Environment - Class or situation in which the whole process is conducted.

The Terminology:

Education is a process of growth, development and adding something new to one's experiences. There are two phases involved in the educational process, namely teaching and learning.

Teaching consists of 'organisation and conduct of learning experience' by the teacher.

Learning is an adjustment of the whole organism by the student to a new situation created by the teacher.

Teacher is a person who stimulates learning in the student by organising and guiding certain experiences of the individuals under his leadership. He is essentially an educator who 'leads out' all that is best in the student.

Student is a person who is desirous of adjusting his whole organisation to a new situation organised and guided by the teacher.

Methods are techniques or procedures used by the teacher through which an interaction between teacher and student takes places.

The Scope of Teaching - Learning :

The purpose of teaching is to induce change in the student. There can be no teaching unless learning takes place. The teacher merely arranges the environment for learning and stimulates and guides the student's activity in the environment. It is the student who learns and each student has to do his own learning. Teaching serves to bring the student into a learning environment and enhance the efficiency of the learning process.

Teaching is a science in the sense that it involves logical and systematic arrangement based on certain principles. Teaching is also an art, meaning that it cannot be reduced to a formula. Teaching as an art requires sensitivity to factors affecting the student and his environment for learning and which must be suitably modified according to his needs.

The whole educational process involving teaching-learning centres round the most important factor - the student.

Methods of Teaching:

During the process of teaching several methods have been tried over many years and we find that they fall into two main categories :

1. Instructional Methods used in the classroom for teaching theoretical subjects; and
2. Methods used for teaching practical skills on the fields or in gymnasiums.

The classroom methods are variously named the lecture method, the recitation method, the project method, the laboratory method, the dramatic method and the group discussion method. The methods for teaching skills or physical activities however, have not been properly categorised. Each method used in the classroom situation has many implications for teaching physical activities and skills, but they cannot be directly applied to teaching physical activities and skills. Even in respect of classroom teaching, no single method or pattern could serve as the best method for all teaching situations. The method of teaching yogic practices comes closer to that of physical activities rather than theoretical subjects.

Traditionally, there have been two approaches towards successful teaching : the first is a teacher-centred approach and the second a student-centred approach.

The teacher-centred approach was the main method in the past, even in Yoga. But today scientific thought focuses its attention on and emphasises the student-centred approach. So naturally, the principles and concepts which underlie the method are expected to involve this student-centred approach, the main emphasis of which is on due consideration of the needs of the students.

Methods of teaching must be compatible with the goals sought or the outcomes expected. The purpose of any method is to create learning in the student. The teacher should know how a particular method he uses affects the student's learning ability. The following are some of the basic methods of teaching:

1) ***Lecture Method:***

It is perhaps the oldest method used for formal teaching. It is valuable in organising large fields on material, separating a particular type of information for immediate use, presenting new information and synthesising information from a wide variety of sources. It is more useful with mature students having a high degree of auditory perception since it involves problems of attention, voice level, clarity, use of rest period and vocabulary level.

The lecture has considerable use in teaching yogic practices. It may be used in presenting any type of information related to particular activity in the perspective of Yoga in general. When extensive lecture is necessary for the achievement of a specific goal, the students should be able to hear the teacher clearly. A lecture can be stimulating, interesting and motivating to the students if the teacher prepares it properly.

The lecture method proves of greater advantage when combined with other methods. The use of visual materials is of considerable help in aiding students to retain the content of the lecture.

When using the lecture method the teacher should also be aware of the limitations of this method, which may be mentioned as follows:

i) It is teacher-centered activity and may encourage lack of participation on the part of the students.

ii) Many students lack ability to learn by this method.

iii) It may lead teachers to ignore more effective methods.

iv) The attention span of more immature students is too short to benefit from a long lecture.

2) Response-to-Instruction Method:

In this method the teacher gives precise instructions which precede, follow or are concurrent with a demonstration and all students respond to the instructions of the teacher in the same way.

There is very little attention paid to the individuals. The emphasis in on the subject matter of activity that is introduced. This method has a formal approach. An information approach with this method is more favorable in teaching such activities where there is some variation in the performance of individuals. This methods can be profitably used after due attention to problems of individuals.

3) Individualized Instructional Method :

It is based on the principle that learning is highly individualized. In this method attempts are made to provide by different means for individual differences within the pattern of the group structure.

4) Group-discussion Method :

Group discussion is an educational technique primarily designed for use in situations where a problem needs solution. It has both individual and group value. It helps the individual to learn to express himself in front of others, be tolerant to the opinions of others and improve his ability to think critically on the issues of a problem. The effectiveness of the group discussion method depends upon the teacher's ability to lead the discussion. Until the students develop skills in leadership and in participation the teacher should serve as a leader.

5) Directed-practice Method:

Assignments for extra practice of selected yogic practices out of class hours enhance skill and performance levels of the students. Necessary introduction along with the preliminary practice of selected yogic exercises like Shirṣhasana, Uddiyana, Kapalabhati, Nauli, Purification process etc. may be done in the class and the efficiency could be developed through out-of-class practice. The students should be encouraged to do out-of-classs practice and the teacher may check the results during subsequent classes and give additional suggestions for further practice. Obviously, the success of this method depends upon motivation of the students and their rapport with the teacher.

6) Project Method:

The aim of this method is to enable the students to put into practice what they have learned in the class. It may also be of help for students to learn related information. When the time is short in the regular schedule the project such as preparing note-books on the yogic practices undergone collection of related material from various sources, preparing models and the exhibits of the yogic practices, planned observations of seminars, conferences, competitions related to yogic activities as well as visits to different well-known Yoga centres represent valuable help to teaching under this method.

7) Demonstration Method:

Demonstration refers to non-competitive type performances with emphasis on skill and form. Demonstrations are of value. It properly directed to both performer and viewer. The Demonstration method describes the organization of the teaching of the class with the sole purpose of public demonstration when concluded. Demonstration method as a technique for the use of the class has some disadvantages. The scope of learning is restricted. It utilises existing talent rather than developing new skills. However, the demonstration method serves as an excellent group method.

Unfortunately, there appears to be no simple formula for selecting the best methods. This depends on the conditions available, such as time, space and equipment. The teacher should have the skill to use a particular method and adapt it to prevailing conditions so that the students receive proper orientation and understanding of the technique and purpose of the method. In other words, a method should always be considered as a means to an end and not the end in itself. The method should allow for individual differences and stimulate both creativity and independent thinking in the students. In Yoga, the teaching method has to eclectic, drawing upon useful vital contributions from several existing methods.

FACTORS INFLUENCING THE METHOD:

The following factors govern the selection of a particular method or combination of methods.

1) Content

We have already seen that the method of teaching depends upon the nature of the subject and that the practical subject requires a different method from the theoretical subject. Even different practical skills require different methods. We know also that the method of teaching skills in Physical Education comes closer to the teaching of yogic practices due to the similarity of content.

2) Previous Background and Experience of the Student:

The method of teaching differs according to the previous experience of the students. Progressive skills cannot be taught to those who have not already mastered basic skills. The teacher can save time and energy by inquiring about student's previous experience in the skill to be learned.

3) The Teacher

Efficiency of method depends on the teacher who uses it. Method itself is neither good nor bad. It turns out to be good in the hands of an able teacher. The teacher does influence the method selected. The teachers have the following qualities which are all reflected through the chosen method.

i) A genuine interest in communication.
ii) Love of the work of teaching.
iii) A willingness to share interest and experiences with others.
iv) An ability to put him or herself in the position of the student.
v) The capacity for understanding expressed in an open, authentic way without blaming or condemning the students.
vi) An attractive personality.
vii) The ability to set a good example through lifestyle and behavior.
viii) A sense of professional responsibility towards the students.
ix) A pleasant, yet commanding voice.
x) The awareness that. "The person in the teacher is more important that the method".

Suitable modifications in the methods depending upon the needs of students and the time framework are possible only when the teacher is conscious of the situation he is handling. The art of teaching on the part of the teacher depends on the suitable modifications in the teaching method routinely used.

4) Facilities

Availability of facilities greatly influences the teaching method. It becomes more efficient with the necessary facilities. In the absence of required facilities the teacher sometimes feels insecure, tense and is unable to give of his or her best. These facilities could be in the form of an adequate space, necessary equipment and congenial atmosphere. For example, if there is no hall for teaching Asanas and the class is required to be conducted on the open ground, the teacher will face the problem of introducing Asanas in the lying position. If there are no water facilities available, purification processes or Kriyas will have limitations for teaching. If the atmosphere is noisy, introduction of meditation techniques will be found difficult.

5) Scientific Principles

An effective teaching method depends on the knowledge of important principles of anatomy, physiology, psychology, pedagogy and Yoga so that the teacher may be flexible in modifying the method. These principles provide sound base for selection and formulation of method.

SOURCES OF TEACHING METHODS

Chapter 4

SOURCES OF TEACHING METHODS

The teacher should be well acquainted with the variety of important principles drawn from education, yogic discipline, psychology of learning, anatomy and physiology in order to formulate good teaching methods.

Yogic Principles:

1) Yogic practices are not "exercises" as we understand the word "exercise". The word exercise is generally applied to vigorous physical movements. Since Yogic practices do not involve vigorous movements any kind of violent action be avoided during Yoga practices.

2) The nature of yogic practices is varied and involves different mechanisms through which the results of particular yogic practices are obtained. The asana, pranayama, bandhas-mudras, kriyas and meditation do not use the same channels for bringing the result of the practices.

3) Asanas - one of the most important and best known of the yogic practices are "static stretching procedures". They should be performed slowly and smoothly in order to influence the tonic system rather than the phasic one. Slackning of effort is required in the practice.

4) The position in a particular asana should be comfortably maintained for some time with least effort. Effortless performance and relaxing as much as possible during the final position are the chief characteristics of the technique of asanas.

5) Pranayamic practices are very different in purpose and technique from the "Breathing exercises". They are supposed to increase oxygen uptake. However, they are considered of little value in the literature of Physical Education.

6) Yogic practices should not lead to undue fatigue. If there is fatigue it should be overcome by the practice of relaxation in Shavasana.

7) All yogic practices should be performed according to one's own capacity and without competition with others.

8) All yogic practices should lead to peace of mind.

9) Any yogic routine should begin with psycho-physical relaxation, centering one's attention as one would in prayer, or actual recitation of some prayers.

Psychological Principles:

1. Interest is the best motivation for learning. The teacher should teach in such a way that students maintain their interest and motivation to learn.

2 Activity is necessary for learning. Learning is a process of experience. Unless the student is involved in the experience of activity he/she may not be able to learn. Therefore, practice is essential, especially for motor-learning or skill-learning. Again it is not mere practice but the correct practice that is important. Complex motor skills require more repetitions of correct practice.

3. All learning has a neural basis. Unless proper neuromuscular co-ordination is formed one cannot expect further developments in any motor skills.

4. For efficient learning the material to be learnt must be within the range of experience and abilities of the learner. Learning is highly individualised and results in progressive changes in behavior. The ability to learn depends upon the innate capacity and previous experiences of the student. All individuals do not learn at the same rate.

5. Learning of motor skills is hastened if the performer is able to grasp an intellectual understanding of the nature of the task before beginning the practice.

6. Regular practice of an activity resulting in pleasure and satisfaction contributes to the most effective learning.

7. Occasional short periods of rest between the practice periods produce superior results in learning motor skills. Brief rest period prevent fatigue in the muscles and the efficiency of the muscles is not decreased.

Anatomico-Physiological Principles:

1. Age and sex are the two important factors determining the anatomico-physiological conditions which need to be considered in the teaching-learning conditions process of motor activities. There are anatomical

differences between the male and the female. One of the main difference to be taken into account is the structure. Women are considered to be weaker in structure generally than men. This means that both bones and ankles are not as strong and their bodies have more fatty tissue. The male body is composed of 41.8% of the body weight of muscle, while the female body has 35.8%. The distribution of fatty tissue is 18.2% of the body weight in males and 28.2% in females. Hence this gives men more muscular strength than women.

2. The muscle strength is proportionate to the amount of fat to muscle tissue. The more fat there is obviously the less efficient are the muscles. Reduction in the fat therefore, contributes to building of muscle strength.

3. The abdominal wall can also be weaker in women from a mechanical point of view. Women's abdominal organs are not firmly situated and the abdominal tone is often lost through childbirth, miscarriages or other reproductive problems.

4. There are differences also in the proportions of the different segments of the spinal column, specially in the lumbar region which affects performance of physical movements. The shorter lumbar and thoracic regions in the female sometimes produce a more pronounced shortening of lower back muscles resulting in lordosis. The lumbosacral angle is also different: 138 in female and 133 in male.

5. The tone of the muscles influences to a considerable extent the posture and functions of the bodily organs of an individual. Muscle tone is a sort of sustained contraction of the muscle fibers. Cultivation of improved muscle tone implies relaxation of undue tensions as well as increase of tone of habitually slack muscles. It is accompanied by an increased awareness of the entire body. One becomes aware of undue tensions in the body and learns to relax more and more when one is attempting to regain proper tone. Improvement of muscle tone brings corresponding improvement in equilibrium, circulation and neuroglandular activity. Static stretching of the muscles contributes to the proper development of muscle tone.

6. Abdominal muscles play an important role in holding the abdominal viscera in place. The tone of the abdominal muscles governs the efficient functioning of the organs situated in the abdominal cavity.

7. Muscle efficiency is lost during long periods of inactivity, especially, if the activity is caused by illness. Under such circumstances any physical activities demanding exertion should be introduced slowly and cautiously.

8. Fatigue is not confined exclusively to the particular muscles exercised, but it spreads through the body as a whole to some degree. Hence to remove the fatigue relaxation of the whole body is desirable.
9. The equilibrium of the body involves muscular co-ordination and proper functioning of the semicircular canals of the internal ears, the eyes. The receptors in the skin and nerve endings in muscles and ligaments around joints.
10. Minimum expenditure of energy is the criterion of simplicity and efficiency in any activity. Vigorous movements consume more energy, while static activities consume less energy.
11. The theory and practice of warming up needs consideration when one engages in vigorous, dynamic and jerky activities. It is not relevant in static activity.
12. The centre of gravity in female bodies is lower than in males. This should be taken into consideration in practices involving stability and balance.

Educational Principles:

1. Learning depends upon impressions received by the necessary receptors. Five senses represent the avenues of learning. Therefore, the presentation of a specific practice of skill should involve as many senses as possible to form an adequate image of the practice.

   However, the most important cues in practice come from audiovisual aids, Motor learning is perceptual, cognitive, rational, thoughtful and involves mental as well as physical aspects of learning. The ideas must be translated into muscular action.

   There are individual differences in effectively utilising various kinds of sensory information. Some individuals have remarkable ability to organise visually presented information quickly. Others synthesise information and analyse the situation, hence appear to respond more slowly.

   Visual demonstration of the practice is one of the most effective ways to enhance the learning of a motor skill. However, the learning is hastened if the student is able to grasp an intellectual understanding of the nature of the task before the beginning of the practice and is given sometimes to integrate the initial cues from observing the demonstration and listening to instructions. Brief, clear descriptions of the activity with repeated demonstrations and pointing out likely faults bring good results.

2. At the preliminary stage, 'overlearning' through repeated practice is necessary. The emphasis should be on aiming at right or correct practice. This can be done by specific instruction. Instructions may also be divided into those offered before the performance of the activity, those which accompany performance and those by way of information or corrections at the end of the performance of the activity.

   Formal instructions are best situated during the initial phases of the learning process. Initial instructions prevent the student from adopting incorrect habits that might later have to be unlearned.

   Students should be instructed in the positive way of performing the activity rather than being informed initially what to avoid. However, best performance comes when individuals are informed both what to do and what to avoid.

   This helps in learning the activity by eliminating possible errors as well as increasing such positive aspects as ease, comfort, efficiency, lowering of tension during performance as speed in some respects.

3. Adequate time should be allotted for actual practice without which learning cannot be effective. The practice period should be divided into informal practice and supervised practice in a group.

4. The Principle of "Progression" is vital to learning. It means performance of any activity from "simple to complex" and "from known to unknown". This principle rests upon a sound neuro-muscular basis. Complex motor learning requires an order or pre-requisites, a background of specific attainments. The learning of coordinated movement patterns is dependent upon the possession of sufficient amount of fundamental physical abilities such as muscular strength, flexibility, muscular endurance and cardio-respiratory endurance. This obvious relationship is sometimes ignored, but effective learning is possible only when this relationship is kept in mind. The whole programme of activities should therefore, be planned and conducted in the light of the principle of progression.

5. Effective learning takes place through the use of the whole Method, Part Method or a Combination of Whole and Part Methods. The combined method is also called Progressive Part Method or Repetitive Part or Continuous Part Method. The uses of any of these methods depend on the degree of complexity of the activity.

a) The whole Method consists in presenting the activity in its entirely without any division. If the activity to be learnt is not complex and the learner is mature, the whole method is suitable.

b) The Part Method is based on analysis of the purpose and of identifying a logical sequence of parts for presentation from simple to complex. The Part Method is better if the student is immature and/or the activity complex.

c) Progressive Part Method is more often used than the part method. In this method a part is learned, paired with the second part and the two practised together. Then the third part is practised and three parts practised as a whole until the entire activity is constructed.

Methods of presentation may stress formal instructions or informal suggestions. But the fundamental basis of all methods is the nature and need of the students, including their individual and group characteristics in learning. The nature of educational objectives and the type of activities use in the programme also dictate the choice of methods.

6. The teacher's interest and attitude towards the students determines to a great extent adequate learning. There is a need on the part of the teacher to inspire the student to accurate and satisfactory performance. If the student is not performing correctly he should be shown the points where he/she makes mistakes in a positive way that encourages self-correction.

7. Learning does not take place unless there is some way for the performer to assess his/her relative success or failure. Although it is necessary to correct faulty performance, too many corrections at a time can confuse. The teacher should correct the most important fault first. Most correction should be in the form of positive suggestions.

8. Immediately after the ideal demonstration of the activity the opportunity to try out and practise the activity should be provided for the students.

9. The teacher should encourage students to ask any questions related the activity, listen to what each person has to say and try to understand his problem. Never discourage or ridicule even a trifling question. It may add to new thinking on the part of the teacher. Give a suitable answer to his satisfaction and/or use the question to open a discussion in the class as a whole if necessary.

Sociological Principles:

1. Utility Value:

The idea of utility need not necessarily be interpreted in the light of activities involved in earning a living alone. Many activities and experiences are of real practical use in helping the person to live happily and successfully that are not of any immediate vocational significance. Yogic practices may not necessarily be of vocational value but they are certainly of immediate practical use for a person of any age and sex in maintaining good health and physical fitness together with happiness in life.

CLASS MANAGEMENT

Chapter 5

CLASS MANAGEMENT

Students rarely cause trouble when they are interested and when suitable lesson content is presented in a competent and stimulating fashion. One essential thing in reducing the problem of control to a minimum is to create an atmosphere of natural freedom, friendliness, mutual help and understanding. There qualities in a class should emanate from the leadership of the teacher. This develops social consciousness in students and awareness of their responsibility to the group.

The students or participants of Yoga may be grouped under the following headings:

a) Beginners
b) Experienced or advanced
c) School Children
d) Special Attention Groups

a) Beginners Group: This group may involve persons of all ages, males and females, young and old and special individuals who are making their first acquaintance with Yoga. They need a general background of yogic discipline and motivation to continue with Yoga.

b) Experienced or Advanced Group : This group may consists of persons who have some experience with Yoga and wish to advance further to gain more varied and deeper experience. Their expectation is to acquaint themselves with a greater number of yogic practices and indulge in subtler and higher practices intensively.

c) School Children: This is a select group ranging from the age of 6 years to 18 years and commands largest percentage of the society. School children need exposure to the field of Yoga based on their immediate needs of their age and temperament.

d) Special Attention Group: These individuals can vary on the basis of age like children and adults; on the basis of sex like males and females;

on the basis of age and sex like boys and girls; on the basis of individual problems of health, abnormality or handicaps. All these individuals need special attention which is possible in a homogeneous group but not in a heterogeneous group.

Dealing with Difficult Students:

The following techniques are useful in dealing with inattentive, talkative or difficult students.

1. Individual students who are disturbing the class may have their attention directed by pausing during instruction, glancing in the direction of the particular student, calling his or her name and asking a question, or if the disturbance is troubling the rest of the class, it should also be pointed out that they are preventing others who are paying attention and working well from hearing the instructions. Alternately, the class can be switched to another activity.
2. It may help to separate people who talk perpetually but if these students continue to cause disturbance after a few warnings, they should be sent out of the class for a short period, However, it is important to bring the person back soon in the class and to let him or her know that improved behavior is expected.

In addition, the teacher will have more control if he or she avoids being too familiar with older students. Be friendly but maintain your dignity and social distance. Remember that you are their teacher.

Also never allow yourself to become antagonistic towards a student. Your effectiveness in helping him will depend upon your patience and understanding.

Seating Arrangement:

The organization of the class may have any suitable form of seating either in lines, rows, a semi-circle or small circle. Consider that each student needs about 40 square feet and arrange your room accordingly. (See Fig.1).

It is preferable if the floor is covered with a carpet but if this is not possible the floor should be clean and each student should use his own mat. In either case it is desirable that the mat or carpet is covered by a clean sheet of cloth of 6 feet * 3 feet.

The seat of the teacher should be such that the teacher is visible to every student. If the group is large, a platform is necessary for the teacher to be visible. In a small group a semi-circle is more suitable as it allows every student to see the teacher clearly. When a platform is used, a revolving one is ideal.

The hall or room where the class is conducted should be well ventilated. It should be well lit so that not only is the class able to see the teacher but the teacher should have a clear view of the class when he is teaching from the platform and while moving about for teaching and answering questions.

The practice room or hall should be as quiet as possible and free from any disturbance.

Instructions:

Learning of a particular Yoga practice depends upon precise instructions by the teacher. Formal instructions are best suited during the initial stage of learning the practice. Instructions could be divided into those that are given verbally before the beginning of the yogic practice, those which accompany performance of the activity individually or by the group and those that are extended by way of information or corrections after the completion of the activity. Initial instructions prevent the student from adopting incorrect habits which might have to be unlearned later. Practical instructions guide the students for correct and efficient performance.

The following guidelines can help the teacher to convey instructions clearly.

i) Be sure that you have the attention of everyone in the class before any instructions are given.

ii) When a long explanation is neeeded it is best to have the class sit down and if necessary closer to the teacher.

iii) Make your instructions brief, perfectly clear and spoken slowly and distinctly.

iv) The instructions should be given for only one thing at a time.

v) Try to use different words and expressions to catch the attention of the students. For example, if students do not understand the first time, use different words in repeating the instructions.

vi) Describe the technique and procedure of any activity before the students are actually asked to practice.

FIG. 1

FORMATION OF THE CLASS

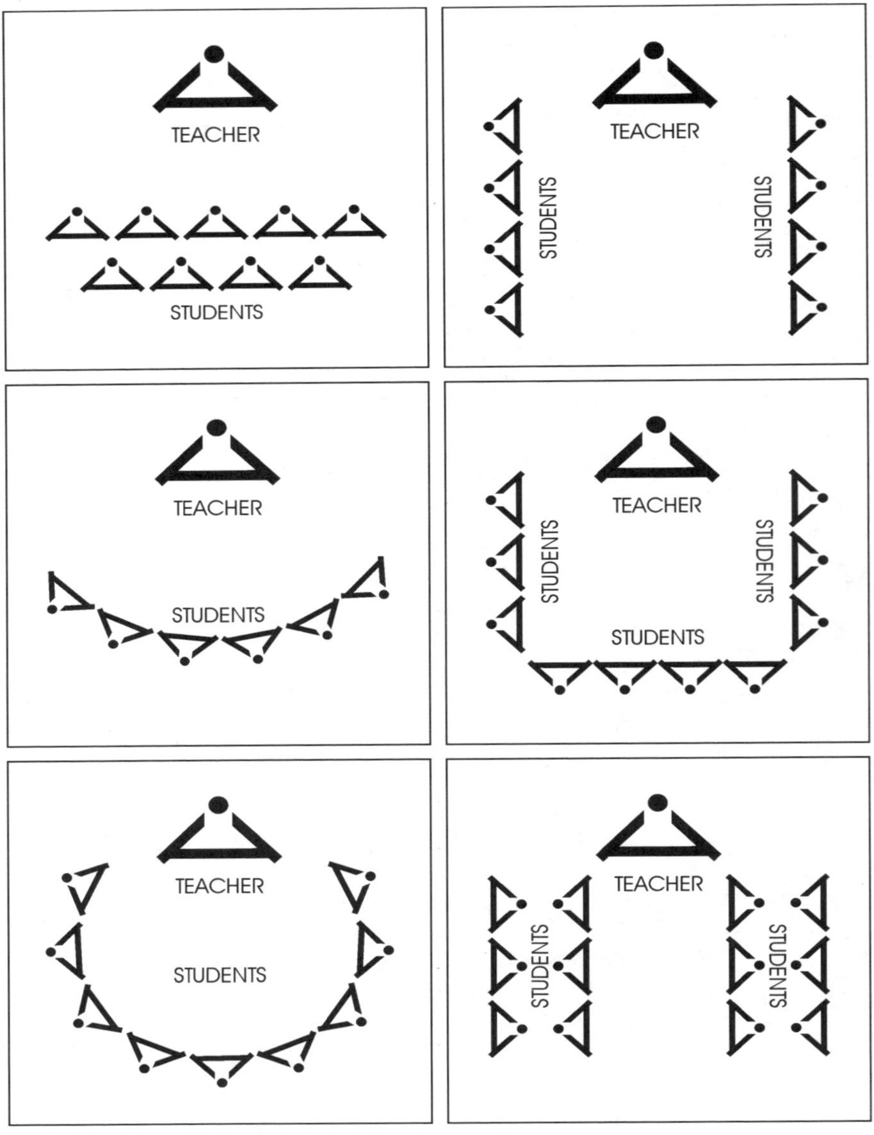

Discussion:

A small question-answer session is very helpful at the end of the lesson to evaluate the outcome and remove any difficulties on the part of the students.

The following hints will be useful in conducting a question-answer discussion session.

i) Encourage the students to ask their questions or address their comments to the group discussion.

ii) Never discourage or ridicule any student's question or contribution whatever small it may be.

iii) Try to draw all students into discussion rather than a few who are always ready to talk.

iv) It is wise to limit the discussion to a few important points.

v) The teacher is expected to know more than the students on the points of discussion. If the teacher is not prepared to answer any question or does not know any point he should not hesitate to say so, and should say that he will find out answer and explain that at the next meeting.

vi) Remember that young children are not mature enough to participate in a group discussion so a different approach is necessary in encouraging them to share their experience.

vii) Exercise some control over the time spent on questions. Steer the discussion to important and relevant questions. Do not sacrifice valuable time on those points that are not important.

Extra - class Practice:

Once the Yoga practice is introduced and techniques explained to the students, it is desirable that they are encouraged to practise on their own at home. All kinds of motivation for the practice at home should be given and they should be assured of all help for correction, modification, improvement from the teacher when they meet next.

THE TEACHING AIDS IN YOGA AND IT'S IMPORTANCE

Chapter 6

THE TEACHING AIDS IN YOGA AND IT'S IMPORTANCE

Mr. Comenius said, "The foundation of all learning, consisting in representing clearly to the senses, sensible objects so that they can be appreciated easily".

The Aids are the powerful means, starters and motivators to understand and learn the subject matter. It is not the end but means to teach in a better way. It is not designed to amuse the students only but to use mostly senses, sight and hearing. It is a very powerful media for better teaching. Modern days, every good teacher uses it.

DIFFERENT TYPES OF AIDS:

A teacher should use maximum possible channels like motor and sense organs through which students can understand the subject matter along with its skill. Even the touch modality may be applied to get better understanding like Uddiyana, Nauli, Agnisara. This modality can be used for the blind people. Various models of yogic practices can be used even for the blind people.

It is to use all possible channels through: 1. The ear like Gramophone, Radio, 2. The Eyes like Picture Movie camera, Black board, Bulletin, Map, Chart, Diagrams, 3. Both eyes & Ears like Sound motion Picture, Television, 4. Activity like educational tour & Travel, 5. Other ways & means like News papers, Books, Yogic dramas.

USING ALL POSSIBLE PICTURES:

It is a known fact that a good picture is worth a thousand words. They say, "Seeing is believing". Therefore, arrangement of the teaching aids is a must in a class situation. Hatha Yoga learning is not an exception to that.

These pictures[1] can be kept hanging for hours together and the teacher can explain the details of them very easily to the students.

Advantages of teaching aids:

Obviously, the learner learns the lessons *quickly* and effectively. It helps the teacher to *motivate* or activate the students in learning the lessons. It keeps the students *busy* and they start *thinking.* The knowledge imparted through this media remains for a *longer* time because of its impression. Due to display and with various aids, the subject matter is much more made *clear* to the students. The desired *objective* of the lesson is quickly fulfilled. The pupils are the best judges whether the aid is *effective* or not. Hence, one as a yoga teacher should know the *basic principles* of preparing the aids.

PRINCIPLES OF SELECTING TEACHING AIDS & THEIR BASIC STEPS

Teacher should select the teaching aid *very carefully* and should be *familiar* with it. There should be *novelty* in the use of teaching aids. It should be *lively*. Too *much use of aids* in a class situation should be avoided. The aid should be prepared in *advance* and *checked* thoroughly before being used or presented. It should be used when the students *are ready* to receive it. It should be *used timely* and should be accurate and technically *excellent*. They should be presented *sequentially*. A *discussion* should be made at the end as to what students have understood through the device. It should not *cost* much.

VARIOUS AIDS USED IN TEACHING:

1) Blackboard 2) Bulletin Board 3) Graphic Devices, 4) Illustrated Text Books[1, 4] 5) Magnetic Board, 6) Yogic Models, 7) Overhead projector, 8) Wall Poster, Charts 9) Yogic Pictures, 10) Tape recorder, Gramophone, Loud Speaker, 11) Television, Video C.D. 12) L.C.D. etc.

The Aids are the powerful means, starters and motivators to understand and learn the subject matter. A teacher should use maximum possible channels through which students can understand the subject matter. Both eyes & Ears like Sound motion Picture, Television. It helps the teacher to motivate or activate the students in learning the lessons. A teacher can keep the chart hanging for hours together and explain the matter. Teacher should select the teaching aid, models very carefully and should be familiar with it. There should be novelty in the use of teaching aids. Blackboard, Bulletin Board, Graphic Devices, Illustrated Text Books[4], Magnetic Board, Yogic Models, Overhead projector, Poster, Charts, Yogic Pictures, Tape recorder, Gramophone, Loud Speaker, Television, Video, L.C.D. etc are a few important aids.

Teacher should use teaching aid regularly in a class situation. He should use at least black-board with stick figures. The impressions created through this media remain for longer time. The teaching aids[3] are the motivators but they can not replace teachers. The teaching aids can be kept displayed through out the class period. The attention of the students is drawn to the subject matter only. The skills are learnt better. The objective of teaching is fulfilled.

Conclusion: The Audio-visual Aids

The progress of science in various fields has developed techniques that have made knowledge widely available. These radically alter our systems of communication. The use of computers, for example, has reduced the need for man-power in the area of teaching. Several groups of students in different locations can be served from a single source which can show the same programme to many different groups. There are many revolutionary possibilities opening up the field of communications through such media as television, video, satellite etc. This is a new phase in our history and these media have immense possibilities for reaching an enormous number of people.

Although sophisticated audio-visual aids are not always within the reach of the teacher, it is necessary to realise the importance of these aids in the learning process. A teaching aid provides quick information about the subject matter to the students. It gives the teacher a better opportunity of conveying the meaning of what he is saying. It helps the students at all levels to grasp the important points in a class situation. It helps to make the lesson interesting and students are more receptive. Hence it is a very important aspect of teaching method. The response of the students is the best way to judge whether the aid is effective or not, but even if the teacher cannot tell this in advance he should, nevertheless, know the basic principles of preparing and using the aids.

The various teaching aids which are mostly used include blackboards, bulletin boards, picture of all kinds diagrams, sketches, drawings, charts, models, projected devices such as filmstrips, slides, motion pictures and recordings, video-cassettes and television.

Visual demonstration is one of the most effective aids to enhance the learning of a motor activity. There are individual differences related to the manner in which various kinds of sensory information is effectively used by the students. Some students have remarkable ability to quickly organise visually presented information. It is desirable that the teacher himself should give the demonstration of a particular Yoga practice. The teacher can communicate with his students better through the demonstration staged by him. At the same time he should verbally explain clearly the fundamental principles underlying the Yoga practice. Any practice by the students must be preceded by visual demonstration to be effective.

ART AND SCIENCE OF QUESTIONING IN YOGA TEACHING

Chapter 7

ART AND SCIENCE OF QUESTIONING IN YOGA TEACHING

Teaching is an art as well as science (Ganguly, S.K.etal.1976). Teaching is a science, because it follows certain scientific principles. It is a systematized branch of knowledge that follows the principles of physiology, psychology, sociology and pedagogy. However, the principles of teaching cannot be reduced into formula as done in mathematical sciences. Teaching is an art because it is a talented and a skillful job on the part of the teacher. Some persons are born teachers as they have an inborn talent in teaching. But an individual can acquire art and science of teaching skill through proper training and practice. Teaching is a science in the sense that it cannot be reduced into a formula. It is a science because it is based on certain principles, which are codified. The objective of a teacher is the effective transfer of knowledge. A flexible approach is important. Motivation and creation of the proper environment are necessary. Learning through the question-answer method is associated not only with other academic subjects but also can be used amply in teaching yogic practices. Right from ancient days, when Muni-Rishis use to teach, the means of teaching was mostly through question and answer method. Even in the Bhagwat Gita (Ramsukhadas, Swami. 2001), one gets the reference of this method, saying "Pariprashena Sevaya" (B.G.: 4:34) meaning through questions and answers, Guru use to clarify the doubts of Sysyas. Out of various methods (Gharote, M.L. and Ganguly S.K. 2001) of teaching, this question-answer method of teaching is the oldest one and very much effective and popular even today. Being one of the means, even from child level to aged students can be taught in a class with this question-answer method to some extent.

AIM OF QUESTIONING

The aim of questioning is to help the teacher to understand the ability of the child and to understand the past and present status of the students.

THE OBJ ECTIVES OF QUESTIONING (Pathak and Tyagi, 1982) :

1. It helps in motivating or activating the students so as to draw his/her attention towards the subject matter.

2. It develops interest and goes on developing question minded which in turn help not to remain idle.
3. Teacher understands the ability of the child and in which subject he takes interest.
4. Teachers understand whether the child has understood his teaching or not. This helps him to go further ahead of the subject.
5. It is to add new knowledge with the old.
6. It allows the child to think and to develop the habit to think.
7. It is to understand the difficulty of the child.
8. If the answers are well received by the teacher, he then can think that his teaching is successful.
9. It is to help the students at various phases of learning.
10. It also helps to develop the mental faculty.

KINDS OF QUESTIONS (Pathak & Tyagi, 1982)

1. Introductory questions:

It is to find the depth and past experience/knowledge of the student and next to add something new into it by creating further interest.

a) To begin with a lesson, Yoga teacher puts an introductory question like what do you mean by Asanas?

b) Only one / two questions should be asked to begin with.

These, in fact help the teacher to develop the child in the lesson/subject matter. The students are compelled to use their brain, rationalize the issue and increase their observation power.

Example from **Agriculture field** like "Cultivation of Cotton":

- How do we cover our body ?
- How are the cloths being prepared ?
- From which tree do we get the cotton ?

Similarly, basing on the above, from yogic teaching point of view, similar questions on Asanas teaching can be asked:

- Why do you want health ?
- Is health necessary for our day-to-day work ?
- Why do you want fitness ?
- Are they necessary in our lives ?
- How can we get health and fitness ?

- What is the aim of Asanas mentioned in traditional texts ?

2. Developing questions:

This helps the teacher to develop the students in the particular study or learning subject mater. The students are compelled to use their brain, rationalize the issue and increase their observation power.

For example, suppose teacher wants to teach about **Calcutta port** from Geography point of view, the question in this context would have been:

a) Where is Calcutta port situated in this map of India ?
b) Which is the place of Calcutta is known as Khidirpur ?
c) Why this place is so thickly populated ?
d) What are those things that are exported from Calcutta port ?
e) Why is Jute famous in West Bengal ?
f) Where are those Jute mills situated ?
g) Why are they established over here ?

So in teaching yoga lesson, a yoga teacher can ask about:

- How many systems are there in this chart of human body ?
- What are their functions ?
- Where is your liver situated ?
- Where is kidney situated ?
- What is the function of it ?
- Is there any relation of this organ to any other organs?
- How many Pranas, Cakras, Nadis, Vital points are there in Yogic Anatomy-Physiology ?
- How do yogic practices work on different systems ?

3. Thought provoking questions :

This is used specially to develop new ideas. More so, the teacher draws maximally the attention of the students and to involve the students maximally by drawing their attention towards the lesson.

Topic from History: **"Akbar and Rajput family relationship"**

- Why did Akbar give top most posts to the Rajputs ?
- Why were they so respected?
- Why did he marry Rajasthani lady?
- From Yoga teaching, a teacher can ask rational on the questions:

- What is relationship of Muscular system and doing of Asanas ?
- What is the relationship of Nervous system and Pranayamic breathing ?
- What could be the sequence in learning different Yogic practices ? Give rational.
- Do we get any reference about it in traditional texts ?

4. Problematic questions :

Just like a topic selected from History regarding World War, a teacher places a problem before the students to solve the same.

What will happen if two great powers – Russia and America fight with each other ?

- What could have been the situation if Hitler would have own the world ?
- Similarly from yogic field like Pranayama in relation to respiratory system could be asked:
- Is Pranayama related to respiratory or Nervous system ?
- Is control of breath Pranayama ?
- Is singing or weightlifting where in one controls breath then be called as Pranayama ?
- Is it because chest expands we breathe in or we breathe in and hence chest expands ?
- Which one is true ?
- Which part of your chest expands more when you breathe in?
- When you breathe in, Abdomen and/or chest, or clavicle or abdomen gets in and chest bulges out ?
- What will happen, if we take out kidney from the body ?

5. Question of comprehension:

This type of question is asked with a view to give good understanding about the lesson that the teacher presents in a class situation. This type of question will gradually increase the grasping power of the students about the topic and the clarity of thinking will be increased.

Topic from History on : **Sikandar and Pauras**

- Why did Sikandar attack India?
- Why did Pauras fight with Sikandar ?

- Why did Pauras lose the war?
- How did Sikandar behave with Pauras ?

A Yoga Teacher can ask question on similar pattern:

- Why should we follow the principals of Asanas ?
- What are the principals of Pranayama ?
- Why bandhas are necessary in Pranayama (Kumbhakas) ?
- How should one practice Asanas ?

6. Comparison questions:

One learns the lesson effectively by way of comparison and thereby differentiating two from each other.

Topic - Way of life or Life pattern.

- How is the weather of Bengal and Punjab ?
- What is the dress of these people ?
- What are the different living patterns of these two people ?
- What are the food patterns of these two people ?

From yogic field questions like :

- What are the difference between Asanas and Exercises ?
- How Mudras are different than Asana ?.
- What are the difference between Normal, Pranayama and Deep breathing?

7. Recapitulatory questions:

It is to revise the whole topic in a class situation. This is asked at the end of the lesson to revise the whole teaching and to test the merit of the students.

Topic - Life style of Kashmiri people.

- How do they dress themselves ?
- What is the main food of these Kashmiris ?
- What is the business of these people ?
- What are the socio-economical patterns of Kashmir ?

Similarly, from Yoga field, a teacher can ask :

l Why do we do Asanas and Pranayama ? What is the role of bandhas and Mudras? How many steps are there in Yoga according to Patanjali Yoga Darshan?

- How many steps are there in Yoga according to Gheranda Samhita?
- How many steps are there in Yoga according to Hathapradipika?

Basic Characteristic of good questions :

To ask question is an art as well as science. There are certain dos and don'ts. It should be short and sweet. By no means should it be lengthy. It should be pin pointed.

1. Question should be asked according to students' age and sex.
2. Ask harder question to matured students and easier to the poor students.
3. Language of the question should be easy. Teacher should not use harder words.
4. All questions should be as such which motivate the child.
5. Questions should be thrown to all and not to any particular students.
6. Question should be meaningful and relevant to the topic.
7. Ask the question politely.
8. Do not attack any student in particular to harass him/her.
9. Do not ask the question quickly. Give the student time to think and interact.
10. Do not ask repeatedly the questions. Change the sentence when repeated.
11. Do not ask yes or no type questions for it could be vague.
12. Do not ask the question only for the shake of questioning.
13. Do not ask incomplete question.

Lastly, while presenting a lesson, the Yoga teacher can do well, if he puts certain questions in a class situation to begin with. So there are number of advantages that are there in it. Hence, a little bit of attention should be paid in this area for it has got various merits. In this way, a teacher can revise the different theoretical subjects like Patanjali Yoga Darshan, Hatha Texts, Cultural Synthesis, Mental Health, and Anatomy-Physiology of Yoga Practices etc. Ultimately the purpose of teaching will be better and the progress in learning will be satisfactory. At no cost, the Yoga teacher should forget this part.

LESSON PLANNING

Chapter 8

LESSON PLANNING

We have seen earlier that the purpose of teaching is to cause desirable change in the student. Successful planning is necessary on the part of a teacher in order to fulfill this purpose. A plan of each lesson should therefore, be prepared.

The advantages of a written lesson plan are :

i) It helps the teacher to organise his thinking.

ii) It increases the teacher's confidence and prevents him or her from losing direction during the lesson.

iii) It helps the teacher to keep the teaching procedure and objectives in minds.

iv) It ensures availability of necessary materials and saves last minute rush to provide adequate arrangements and anxiety caused by such a situation.

v) It serves as an aid for future plans.

Essentials of a Good Lesson Plan :

1) It should be prepared shortly before use.
2) It should be specific and detailed.
3) It should take cognisance of individual differences.
4) It should include (a) statement of objectives of the lesson, (b) statement materials needed, (d) description of method and procedures to be used, (e) provisions for linking previous and future plans to be used, (f) provisions for comments by the teacher after the lesson.

Whatever the type of method selected for teaching it should be compatible with the purpose or desired outcome and the best among available methods to bring the desired outcome. It should be adapted to the activity to be taught. It should also be feasible taking into consideration time, space and equipment available. The teacher should have the skill to use a particular method. Proper orientation and understanding of the technique and purpose of the method should be given to the students.

The immediate goal of any yogic lesson is to introduce a particular Yoga practice and its correct technique and give the feel of that practice to the participants of the lesson so that they are motivated to continue further practise and derive maximum benefits. In order to attain these objective the yogic lesson should be properly planned and executed.

Here are some guidelines for conducting Yoga lessons successfully :

1. ***Setting the Atmosphere:*** A Yoga class should begin with a calm and quit atmosphere. It may start with a short prayer or with a prayerful mood. As far as possible some meditative pose may be recommended for this purpose. The students are asked to take their seats in a suitable formation. The quit sitting or prayerful mood creates suitable internal environment in the students conducive to the yoga lesson.

2. ***Introduction to the Practice:*** The main part of the lesson starts with the introduction of the Yoga practice. This introductory part may be divided into two sections. The first part may be devoted to verbal instructions with the background of the practice containing as much information about the practice as possible. This part is specially intended to create interest and motivation among the students. Depending upon the knowledge of the teachers about the practice and his/her skill in presenting the information, the teacher can make this part more interesting and motivating.

3. ***Demonstrating Practices:*** The second part may be devoted to the ideal demonstration of the Yoga practice as a whole. Although it is possible to take the help of Audio-visual aids like pictures, sketches, filmstrips etc. It is more impressive, practical and desirable that the demonstration is staged by the teacher himself. As far as possible this demonstration should be most efficient faultless and complete so that an overall image of the practice is presented to the students. As compared to the presentation of a particular Yoga practice through an audio-visual means, when the teacher himself demonstrates the practice the students can relate personally to the teacher and identify more closely with the practices shown. There is more appreciation and respect for the teacher generated through live demonstration.

4. ***Analyzing the practice*** : The whole demonstration of the Yoga practice may be useful in forming an overall general picture. But it may not be

enough to get into the detailed stages of the technique which requires analysis of that practice. The insight into the proper technique is gained only be analysing the practice in its various parts and then demonstrating them. The analysis of the Yoga practice is more essential when the technique is difficult. When the practice is simple a demonstration as a whole would be sufficient and the analysis may not be necessary. When the practice is analysed and demonstrated in parts, it is desirable to supplement it with a brief and clear description about technique, bringing to the notice of the students salient points of the practice. These salient points should include hints about do's and don'ts.

5. ***Students' Individual Practice Time:*** When students see a technique demonstrated, they naturally want to try it out themselves. So allot some time for the students to try it on their own individually and to find out for themselves how successfully they are able to practise it.

   While students are practising the teacher should watch their performance and find out their difficulties, mistakes and deviations from the correct and ideal performance of the practice. He should correct the most obvious mistakes of those students who are practising in a way that is detrimental to them and then point out common mistakes that are committed generally. A repeat demonstration of the practice as a whole and in parts should be given to ensure that the point of the corrections has been understood by everyone.

6. ***Group Practice:*** After getting the feel of the practice and becoming conversant with the technique the teacher may ask the whole group of students to perform the practice together under the guidance of the teacher in a formal manner. Collective participation in the group will given an idea to the individual about his performance in relation to the performance of others.

7. ***Correcting Mistakes:*** Performance in the group by the students helps the teacher to locate any performance that has deviated from normal and which needs correction. This saves the time of the teacher in checking every individual's performance. He can concentrate on the particular students who are not performing the technique properly. He can suggest necessary modifications in the performance of the students or suggest some lead-up practices in case of particular individuals, if necessary. Yoga practices being essentially individualistic, when they are performed by the group, individual capacities should be taken into consideration.

8. ***Giving Instructions:*** In the group practice when directions are used, it should be remembered that their purpose is to suggest different stages of practice to be undergone in succession by the group. The commands or instructions should, therefore, have a very slow rhythm so that the jerky, motions in response to brisk instructions are avoided and due respect is given to the individual capacities. The emphasis should be on an informal way of performance rather than a formal one.

9. ***Repeat Demonstration:*** The performance of the Yoga practice by the group should be followed by pointing out the lacunas still remaining in the performance of some individuals, suggesting proper corrections and avoiding the mistakes committed by the individuals and elaborating on some points which need clarification or explanation.

10. ***Repeat Practice:*** The group should then repeat the practice of the technique.

11. ***Repeat Demonstration:*** The teacher should demonstrate and clarify the main points again.

12. ***Rest Periods:*** After the group practice is over the students may be given rest in the form of Shavasana- the yogic way of relaxation.

When more than one Yoga practice is introduced, it is desirable that Shavasana is practised at the end of the lesson and sometimes even after some Yoga practices during the lesson, if necessary.

Before the end of the lesson the teacher would do well to sum up points considered as important for the correct and efficient performance of Yoga practice. He could also induce students to ask any questions related to the practice so that there is a good imprint the introduced Yoga practice on the memory of the students.

To sum up the precise steps in the conduct of a yogic lesson, the whole process includes-

1. Creating an environment suitable for the lesson by a prayer or prayerful mood.
2. Establish the concept of Yoga practice be verbal introduction.
3. Giving the complete picture of the Yoga practice through whole demonstration.
4. Analysing the whole performance into suitable parts or stages.

5. Allotting time for getting the feel of the practice by individuals.
6. Group practice under the guidance and supervision of the teacher.
7. Detection and correction of the mistakes in the performance.
8. Giving instructions with emphasis on the salient points analysing the performance again.
9. Giving complete demonstration with clear explanation of the various stages involved in the practice.
10. Again practice by the group.
11. Again providing complete picture of the whole practice by demonstration, discussion, modifications when necessary, lead-up practices for weaker students.
12. Giving complete rest in Shavasana at the end.

Success of the teacher lies in how best he utilizes the above steps in his lesson. Remember, 'Teaching is what you make it.'

The above mentioned ideas or considerations relate to the yoga lesson where new practice is introduced. But a yoga lesson could also be a practice session. Previously introduced practices are undergone during such a lesson. There would obviously be some difference between the two types os yoga lesson. The main purpose of the first type of lesson would be to teach new practice with all details of its technique. The second type, on the other hand emphasises the continuing practice of those techniques already learnt, so that the original techniques are not forgotten and their appropriate health benefits are derived. In the practice type of yoga lesson -

i) There are groups of yogic practices undergone.

ii) The practices are meaningfully chosen from amongst the known techniques.

iii) There is some sequence based on the principle of progression.

iv) As far as possible variety of the groups of yogic practices are chosen for giving maximum benefits through stretching, relaxation, breathing techniques and meditation.

The practice lesson should also follow the pattern given earlier, where the lesson begins with a clam and quit mood and ends with general relaxation with Shavasana or meditation, so that the ultimate experience is given to the participants in the lesson.

A yoga lesson could be also a mixture of the above two types. After having conducted a practice lesson for some time, the teacher could switch to the introduction of the new practice along a similar pattern to the one discussed earlier.Emphasis in advanced groups in practice session could be on a meditative mood throughout the lesson or more time could be devoted to practice of meditation at the end.

SOME HINTS FOR CONDUCTING A LESSON ON MEDITATION

"Meditation is a mental device that limits stimulus input by directing attention to a single unchanging or respective stimulus". Throughout recorded history it has been used to after state of consciousness. It forms a part of religious practices. Recently Meditation has been used for therapeutic purpose rather than as a religious practice. Meditation can be used as a noncultic practice.

The technique of Meditation is related to the biofeedback techniques and to the relaxation methods.

Characteristics of Meditation:

1. During meditation one gets profound rest for the body and mind. Oxygen consumption can be lowered during 20-30 minutes of meditation to a degree which can be reached after 6-7 hours of sleep.
2. Heart and respiratory rates typically decrease.
3. There is a shift to parasympathetic dominance.
4. There is a lowering of anxiety at this time.
5. During Meditation EEG shows an alert-drowsy pattern with high alphas and occasional theta wave patterns as well as unusual pattern of swift shifts from alpha to slower (more sleep-like) frequencies and then back again.
6. Meditation has been physiologically termed as "wakeful, hypometabolic state".
7. When practised regularly it appears that Meditation alters behavior suggesting number of beneficial changes.

Cautions:

Meditation has its limitations. All persons cannot practise meditation even for 20 to 30 minutes. Overdose of meditation for such persons can be dangerous. The theory of "More the better" cannot be applied here.

Release of certain emotions that is difficult to handle may occur with prolonged meditation. In a person with an adverse psychiatric history, the beginning of meditation has been known to precipitate psychotic episodes. Even in relatively stable people, it is probably unwise to introduce prolonged sessions of meditation. To avoid such difficulties meditation should be practised in moderation. It would be beneficial to start the practice of meditation after some amount of practice in stretching like Asanas, rhythmic breathing like pranayama and relaxative technique like Shavasana.

It is doubtful whether meditation can really be ever taught effectively. In fact the state of meditation results out of the background prepared through variety of means contributing to a "meditative mood" which lasts not too long.

The Method of Teaching Meditation:

The method of teaching meditation, therefore, requires creating an atmosphere of tranquility through pleasant voice and simple techniques leading to a meditative mood. All the yogic practices contribute to the building up of the meditative mood. Rather than introducing mechanical technique of meditation the participants be brought to "meditative mood" and left there for a comfortable time, the time being determined by the individual according to his capacity.

It is therefore, desirable that meditation should be introduced alongwith the group of yogic practices rather than as an isolated technique, so that it becomes more beneficial and less harmful. It should be remembered that in the hierarchy or yogic practices meditation occupies a higher position than other practices. However, all yogic practices are complementary to each other and each practice contributes to similar effects on a greater or a lesser scale, Stable, comfortable and erect sitting with head, neck and trunk in a vertical line and regulated breathing facilities the practice of meditation.

Swami Kavalayananda in Meditative Posture

Self Evaluation by the Teacher:

When the teacher continually teaches the same activities in the same manner the teaching loses its interest within a very short time. There should be an appropriate change in the activities and the manner of introducing them which are based on constant evaluation of the teaching by the teacher himself to see where it falls short. In the evaluation the teacher should ask himself such questions as whether he puts enough time and thought on planning lessons that have purpose and progression; whether his students respond enthusiastically; whether he has had a new experience in teaching; whether he could improve upon what he is doing with different procedures and organization; whether he could give more time and attention to the students who lack behind up skills; whether the students improve in their performance in general. A progressive teacher should always experiment with his teaching and constantly evaluate it to become a lively teacher teaching to the satisfaction not only of his students but to the satisfaction of his own self.

MODEL OF LESSON PLANS

MODEL OF LESSON PLANS

NOTES ON YOGIC PRACTICE TEACHING LESSON

Lesson No.: Date :

Name of the Teacher : SKG.

Name of the School : Teachers Training Certificate in Yoga Standard Period 20 Minutes Time

Practice previously introduced : Bhujangasana, Ardha Shala-bhasana, Paschimatanasana, Chakrasana, Shavasana.

Aim of the Lesson : To make the students physically fit, mentally alert and emotionally balanced

Objectives of the Lesson : To acquaint the participants with the Technique of VAKRASANA and to bring about flexibility of spinal muscles and joints, thereby contributing to the flexibility in general.

Equipment Required : NIL.

Stages	Methods
1) **Start of the Lesson** Prayer	: The students are advised to take comfortable sitting pose and to recite the prayer collectively.
2) **Introduction of the Activity** :	
a) Sitting Arrangement	: The same sitting arrangement is maintained for the introduction of the activity.
b) Verbal introduction activity	: The teacher gives verbal the introduction of of the VAKRASANA on

the following points :

i) Importance of spine in the maintenance of health.

ii) Contribution of previously introduced Asanas in cultivation of flexibility of spine.

iii) Special feature of Vakrasana in the contribution of flexibility - Significance of name - Modified easy version of traditional Matsyendrasana.

c) Demonstration in full and in parts : The teacher demonstrates the Vakrasana in full using the following techniques :

i) Sitting with legs extended and hands by the side.

ii) Bending the left leg and placing the left foot by the side of right knee.

iii) Left hand placed at the back in line with spine at a comfortable distance.

iv) Crossing the right hand over the raised knee and placed on the ground.

v) Turning the trunk left ward, looking as far back as possible.

After returning to the original position in reverse order, similar stages are undergone on the right side.

d) Emphasis on the salient points

i) Place the foot by the side of the knee.

ii) Sit straight.

iii) Place the backward hand at a

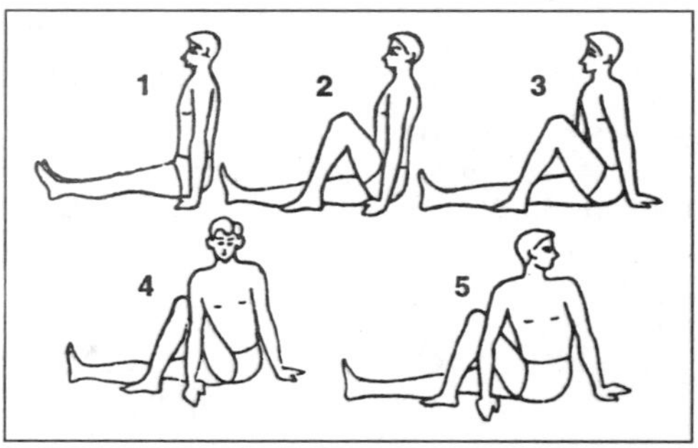

comfortable distance.

iv) Place firmly with the crossed hand against the raised knee.

e) Instruction : The whole process should be smooth and without jerk and should be repeated on both sides.

3) Individual Practice:

i) Allotment of time : The students are asked to perform the asana as demonstrated to them keeping in mind the above instructions. They are suggested to maintain the final position comfortably for some time according to their capacity.

ii) Detection and correction of mistakes : The performance of every studentis carefully observed and the errors in the practice detected and corrected.

4) Group Practice: :

i) Allotment of Time : The instructions are given at every step to make the students practice VAKRASANA as a group under the supervision of the teacher. The optimum time is chosen for maintenance of the final position.

ii) Detection and correction of mistakes : Performance of the individual in the group is watched and the mistakes detected in the group. The group is made aware of the errors so that they should avoid them in the next performance.

5) End of the Lesson:

i) Relaxation : Soon after the group practice the students are instructed to lie down and relax in Shavasana.

ii) Question & Answer : The students are encouraged to ask any doubts or questions about the performance of the Asana and are subsequently answered by the teacher.

NOTES OF YOGIC PRACTICE TEACHING LESSON

Lesson No.:	Date :
Name of the Teacher	: S.K.G.
Name of School	: G.S.C.Y.& C.S.
Standard Last Time	: College, period : : 3.00 p.m. to 3.20 p.m
Practice previously introduced	: Padmasana, Ujjayi, Shavasana, Omkar.
Practice to be introduced	: Surya Bhendana (Without Kumbhaka)
Aim of the lesson	: To give the feeling of tranquility at psychophysiological level
Objective of the lesson	: To teach the technique of Suryabhedana Pranayama.
Equipment Required	: Black board, Chalk, Chart/Poster.

Stages	Methods
1) START OF THE LESSON:	
a) Sitting Arrangement	: The students are asked to sit in a and semicircle and take any meditative posture. They recite their usual prayer.
b) Previous practice	: After the prayer, the students are asked to perform ten rounds of Ujjayi as per the technique previously introduced. The important points of the practice are once again revised by the teacher. The teacher checks the performance of the students for correctness and makes useful suggestions if necessary. After the performance they are asked to listen to the instructions of the teacher.

2) INTRODUCTION OF THE ACTIVITY:

a) Verbal Introduction : The teacher recalls the salient points of the practice of Pranayama in general. Connecting with the previous experience and knowledge of Ujjayi the teacher introduces new practice of Suryabhedana. He gives verbal introduction on the following points.

i) Importance of breathing.

ii) Significance of nostril breathing as compared to oral breathing.

iii) Explanation of the concept of Surya and Chandra related to breathing from a particular nostril.

iv) Use of particular fingers for closing nostrils.

v) Special feature of Surya-bhedana as compared to other varieties of pranayama.

b) Technique (Stages) : Starting Position: Sitting straight in Padmasana or in any meditative posture.

1. Close the index and middle finger of the right hand and place the small and ring finger on the left nostril. The right thumb is placed over the bridge of nose.
2. Close the left nostril by small and ring finger and start inhaling through right nostril.
3. Now close the right nostril with thumb and open the left nostril.
4. Exhale through left nostril slowly taking double the time of inhalation. This completes one round.
5. Again close the left nostril with last two fingers and open the right nostril by withdrawing the thumb.

6. Inhale through right nostril Closing the right nostril exhale slowly through the left. This completes second round. Practice such 4 or 5 rounds.
7. Remove the hand from nose and place it on knee comfortably.

c) Salient Points : The teacher explains salient points for the facilitation of the practice of Suryabhedana in the form of Do' and Don'ts.

Dos	Don'ts
1. Puraka and Rechaka Should be done slowly	1. Avoid doing Suryabhedana if the ratio of 1:2 appears to be difficult.
2. Puraka and Rechaka should be done through nose only.	2. Don't bend in the trunk during the practice.
3. Keep a ratio of 1:2 in Puraka and Rechaka respectively.	3. Don't continue the practice if felt tension/heat in the body.
4. Keep the abdomen in controlled condition.	4. Avoid contour on the face either in Puraka or in Rechaka.
5. Do the activity in sitting condition preferably in Padmasana.	5. Don't produce any sound during inhalation or exhalation.

d) Advantages :

1. Helps to release mental tension.
2. Helps in controlling emotions.
3. Improves blood circulation.

e) Caution :

1. People having high blood pressure should not perform.
2. Person with excessive heat in thebody should not do it.
3. It should not be performed in summer season.

3) a) INDIVIDUAL PRACTICE	:	After giving the above theoretical and practical information, the students will be asked to practice 5 rounds of the Suryabhedana Pranayama.
b) DETECTION AND CORRECTION OF MISTAKES	:	The students' performance will be checked properly and the mistakes will be corrected.
4) a) **GROUP PRACTICE**	:	The teacher will give instructions according to which all the students will be asked to perform 10 rounds of Suryabhedana. The students will be asked to take rest either in Shavasana or in Makarasana for a few minutes.
b) DETECTION AND CORRECTION OF MISTAKES	:	The mistakes committed by some students in the group will be brought to their notice and will be corrected by proper demonstration again by the help of a good student or by the teacher himself.
5) QUESTION-ANSWER	:	The students will then be encouraged to ask questions on the points that they did not understand well. The doubts will be clarified by the teacher. The teacher will also ask a few questions to students to get an idea about the adequate learning of the practice by the students.
6) END OF THE LESSON	:	The teacher will then end the lesson with "OM' recitation for three times and a silence for two minutes. The students then will be asked to open their eyes. The next lesson is announced before the class departs.

NOTES OF YOGIC PRACTICE TEACHING LESSON

Lesson No.	:	Date :
Name of the Teacher	:	S.K.G.
Name of the school	:	T.T.C.C.Y.
Standard	:	College Students,
Period	:	Morning Time : 9.00 To 9.20 A.M.
Practice previously introduced	:	Padmasana, Uddiyana, Ujjayi, Shavasana.
Practice to be introduced	:	Agnisara Kriya
Aim of the Lesson	:	To make the students physically fit, mentally alert and emotionally balanced
Objectives of the Lesson	:	To make the students with the technique of Agnisara and give the benefit of practice on the form of removing abdominal congestion and increase gastric fire.
Equipment Required	:	Chart and posters, Black-board.

Stages		Methods
1) START OF THE LESSON:		
a) Sitting Arrangement and Prayer	:	The participants are asked to take any comfortable sitting posture in a semicircle. The usual prayer is recited with closed eyes for creating calm and quiet atmosphere which is most conducive to yogic practices.
b) Previous Practice	:	Students are asked to stand with legs open and practise three rounds of Uddiyana which was previously introduced. The teacher once again brings to the notice of the students salient points before the starting of the practice. After the practice

is over students are asked to sit comfortably and listen to the instructions of the teacher.

2) INTRODUCTION OF THE ACTIVITY:

a) Verbal Introduction : The teacher gives verbal information about the Agnisara - a new practice to be introduced. He explains the nature, technique and importance of the practice taking into consideration the following points:

i) The concept of purification in Yoga-various modes and methods used.

ii) Significance of Dhauti as a purification process and various forms of Dhauti.

iii) Classification of Agnisara as a Dhauti - its meaning and traditional description.

iv) Respiratory process involved in Agnisara as different from that of Uddiyana.

v) Significance of Agnisara in promoting digestion and assimilation.

b) Demonstration of the in full : The teacher demonstrates the technique Agnisara in full using the following steps :

i) Stand erect with feel apart.

ii) Bend the knees and place the hands on them.

iii) Exhale deeply and hold the breath out.

iv) Vigorously contract the abdominal muscles.

v) Without inhalation push the abdomen forward making it tight.

vi) Repeat contraction and protrusion of the abdomen slowly number of times, holding the breath out.

vii) Inhale and stand erect.

c) Emphasis on salient	:	The teacher invites attention of points the students to the following salient points : i) The practice is done during the condition of breath held out. ii) There is no attempt at raising of the chest or to inhale. iii) Keep the abdominal muscles tight throughout contraction and protrusion.
d) Contraindication	:	The practice of Agnisara should be avoided in conditions of abdominal pain, menstruation and pregnancy.
e) Advantages	:	i) Helps to improve the tone of the abdominal muscles. ii) Improves function of the abdominal organs. iii) Promotes peristaltic movement.
3) INDIVIDUAL PRACTICE	:	The students are then asked to try the performance of Agnisara on their own to get the feel or the practice. The teacher watches their performance keenly and tries to help & correct the performance of some students. If necessary, once again, the teacher can give demonstration to get proper insight into the practice for the students.
4) GROUP PRACTICE	:	All the students perform the practice together as per the instructions and under supervision of the teacher. If there is any faulty performance by some students, it is corrected by the teacher. He again emphasises the salient points of the practice so that the students practise correctly. After desired number of rounds of the practice, the students are asked to lie down and take rest in Shavasana.
5) QUESTION-ANSWER	:	If there are any doubts about the practice the students are encouraged to ask

		questions to which the teacher gives satisfactory answers.
6) END OF THE LESSON	:	The students will be asked to sit comfortably with close eyes and collectively recite the OM sound. Then the class will come to an end.

NOTES OF YOGIC PRACTICE TEACHING LESSON

Lesson No.	:	Date :
Name of the Teacher	:	S.K.G.
Name of the school	:	G.S.C.Y.S.
Standard : College, Period	:	Last Period, Time : 3 to 3.45 pm
Practice previously introduced	:	Padmasana, Shavasana, Ujjayi,
Practice to be introduced	:	Uddiyana Bandha
Aim of the Lesson	:	To make the students towards sound psychophysiological health through the practice of Uddiyana Bandha.
Objectives of the Lesson	:	a) To acquaint the pupils with the technique of Uddiyana bandha. b) To give suitable exercise to the organs in the abdominal cavity.
Equipment Required	:	Anatomical chart of Respiratory system.

Stages		Methods
1) START OF THE LESSON:		
a) Sitting Arrangement and prayer	:	Students are asked to sit in a semi circle in their comfortable positions. The usual prayer is collectively recited with closed eyes.
b) Previous Practice	:	Then they are asked to revise the previous practice of Ujjayi. They practise 10 rounds of Ujjayi breathing.
2) Introduction of the Activity :		
a) Verbal introduction of the New Practice	:	The teacher explains the mechanism of breathing with help of the chart of pictures

with special reference to the movement of the diaphragm in Ujjayi breathing. He explains the relationship of pranayamic breathing with adoption of Mudras and Bandhas. In this connection he explains the significance and utility of Uddiyana Bandha by highlighting on the following points :

i) Significance of the name and its eulogy in the traditional texts.

ii) The concept of mockinhalation as a technique to be followed and its physiological explanation.

b) Full Demonstration : The teacher himself then gives the demonstration following the stages as below :

i) Stand erect with feet apart.

ii) Lean forward and place hands on the knees.

iii) Exhale fully and hold the breath out.

iv) Raise the ribs and expand the chest without inhaling the air.

v) Relax the abdomen and allow it to assume concavity.

vi) Lower the ribs and slowly inhale.

vii) Remove the hands from the knee and stand erect.

c) Salient Points : He brings to the notice of the students following points of importance

i) Keep the shoulders down.

ii) Exhale as deeply as possible.

iii) Practise it only on empty stomach.

iv) Avoid practice during the condition of abdominal pain or cardiovascular disturbance.

d) Advantages : i) Improves blood circulation in abdominal and thoracic region.

		ii) Increases respiratory efficiency. iii) Remove constipation iv) Improves functions of the abdominal organs.
3) Individual Practice	:	Students are asked to try the practice on their own. The teacher observes the performance and helps the students to get the proper technique by pointing out the mistakes of some of the students. He suggests the students to close their nose after complete exhalation and then try to inhale with close nose. When the students get concavity in the abdomen their attention is drawn to it. Next attempt is suggested to be done without closing the nose with hands.
4) Group Practice	:	The teacher then asks the students to practise Uddiyana under his instructions and supervision. The mistakes are again detected and corrected by the teacher. The students are then asked to lie down and rest in Shavasana.
5) Question-Answer	:	The students are asked if they have any questions which are satisfactorily answered by the teacher.
6) End of the Lesson	:	The teacher suggests the extra practice of Uddiyana at home so that the students are able to perform better next time when they meet.

SPECIMEN OF THE NOTES AND OBSERVATIONS OF YOGIC PRACTICE LESSONS

Lesson No. :———————————————————— Date : ——————

Name of the Teacher : ——————————————————————————-

Name of the school : ——————————————————————————

Standard : ——————————— Period : ——— Time ——————

Practice previously introduced : ————————————————————

Practice to be introduced : ———————————————————

Aim of the Lesson : ——————————————————————————
———————————————————————————————————

Objective of the Lesson : ——————————————————————
———————————————————————————————————

Equipment Required : ————————————————————————
———————————————————————————————————

Stages Methods

1) Start of the Lesson

2) a) Introduction of the Activity :

a) Sitting Arrangement :

b) Verbal Introduction :

c) Demonstration and use of Audio-visual Aids

d) Technique demonstrated and explained in stages

e) Salient Points :

f) Advantages :

g) Caution:

3) a) Individual practice :

b) Detection and correction of mistakes :

4) a) Group Practice :

b) Detection and correction of mistakes :

5) Question-Answer :

6) End of the Lesson :

OBSERVATIONS :

1) Planning and Preparation:

2) Presentation :

a) Introduction and Teaching of the Practice (Demonstration, Analysis, Teaching, Detection and Correction of faults, repetition etc.)

b) Technicalities (Instructions, Class arrangement, Teacher's Position, Procedures etc.)

c) Teaching Aids used :

d) Personality, class control etc. :

3) Response of the class :

4) Other Remarks:

5) Viva-Voce:

Date: Signature of the Supervisor

Guideline to organise *Non-residential* Yoga camp.

To organize Yoga camp[7], the following things should be considered and to be seen well in advance and to be followed before yoga camp is organized. Hence, the following points to be kept in mind in advance. However, by no means, this guide line is sufficient and complete one. It changes according to various places of the camps to be organized. ***Therefore, this guideline intends to outlines the ideas on how to plan for organization, administration, and supervision point of view and successfully run a free yoga camp in a city. This camp aims to develop and spread awareness of health oriented physical fitness and mental health. Doing yoga reduces stress and increases concentration. Therefore, it is strongly recommended for Yoga practices as evident through research[8] studies. The camp will be organized for normal healthy persons. The camp in charge should survey well in advanced the place of yoga camp from facilities point of view as mentioned below. A nominal fee may be revived from the participants. An application should be made well in advance to get grant from UGC./Ayush,/ MHRD or any other funding agencies in this regard. For any clarification, the participants should be advised to contact Camp in charge.*** **To organize Yoga camp, the following things should be considered and to be seen well in advance and should be followed before yoga camp is organized. Hence, the following points to be kept in mind in advance. However, by no means, this guide line is sufficient and complete one. It changes according to various places of the camps to be organized.**

Therefore, this article intends to outlines the ideas on how to plan for organization, administration, and supervision point of view and successfully run a free yoga camp in a city for general health.

1. **Advertisement: must be made a month ago in popular Hindi and English local Newspapers especially on Saturday and Sunday edition.**

- ***Duration*** **of programme:** ***Yoga camp*** **for 21 Days from 21st October to 12th.November**
- **Time: from 6AM. to 7AM. and 5 PM. to 6PM.**
- ***The place*****: The address of the Yoga camp to be organized including mobile no. for contact is to be mentioned in the Newspapers.**
- Age Limit: Anybody above the age of 18 years up to 45 Years can participate.

2. ***Medicine*****: Common medicines and first aid are to be kept for emergency.**
3. ***Sunday will be observed as holiday.***
4. **Facilities:**

    - Market place: There should be a market place nearby to purchase for daily use.
    - ***Accommodation*****: Three rooms attached to the practical hall for 5-teaching staffs and for fifty Participants (Ladies and gents),**
    - ***facilities of Water supply*** **both for toilet, bath and drinking and cooking purpose,**
    - ***Staffs:*** **3 gents, 2 ladies, including one medical doctor.**
    - ***Doctor:*** **The Same doctor for the teaching as well as for evaluating the health status of the participants be used before and after the camp starts.**
    - ***Yoga Mats*** **of one's length say 6 feet X 4 feet each which participant will bring.**

- *Mess and cooks*: **There should be one local cook and one helper for cooking arrangement along with utensils, soap, candles, oils, books, etc. for the teaching staff.**
- *Electricity:* **Sufficient facilities for electricity and electricity points should be there in the hall.**
- **Yoga Charts, Blackboard, Overhead projector to be there for the class.**

5. *Timetable for class*: **According to season, a suitable timetable for regular class both for morning and evening are to be made in advance and to be displayed at the camp site as well as in Newspapers. Organization of classes daily should be one in the morning and one in the evening session be conducted there. Whatever taught in the morning practical classes, it should be repeated in the evening class with the addition of a few new practices.** ***This is for the information to all the participants (both ladies and gents) participating in the Nonresidential "Yoga Camp" will be organized in the campus of National stadium. New Delhi from 10th. October to 1st. November 2023-at 6:00am to 7.00am and 5/00pm. to 6/00pm.The participants should carry their own yoga mat, loose yoga wear along with a water bottle.***
6. ***Contra indication: During the menstrual period. the ladies should forgo the training programme.***

7. *Telecommunication facility:* **Two mobiles to be kept exclusively for the 0rganization of camp.**

8. *A counter for Enquiry cum Published yoga books* **to be placed beside the entrance of the yoga practical hall for ready reference.**

9. *Contact with Local Police,* **and senior citizen of that locality for protection and necessary information.**

Apart from teaching staffs, there should be two such local people, who can work for assistance. They will handle all the various and somewhat small details like a liaison between camp in charge/ yoga teacher and the students. *It is always better to take feedback from the participants to note for the future.* **At the end of the yoga camp, a general get together of one hour be arranged in the presence of a VIP, local invitees and yoga experts to get the feedback of the participants along with some photographs of the camp activities.**

FORM TO BE FILLD by the PARTICIPANTS first day of the camp IN THE PRESENCE OF MEDICAL OFFICER (GENERAL INFORMATION):

- Name: ______________________ __________
- Age: ____
- Address: ________________________
- Sex: M/F________________________
- Marital status: _____________________
- Occupation______________________
- Monthly income: _________________
- Family liabilities: _________________
- Physical Exercise (Nature and duration): Nil / Walking/Games/Yoga/Athletics/any other
- History of past illness/operation: _______________________

- Treatment previously taken/results: ______________________________
- Reason for coming to Yoga class and expectation: ______________________________

FAMILY HISTORY:

No. of members in the family: _____________
State of health of other members of the family and ailments: ___________________

HISTORY OF PRESENT ILLNESS:

- Nature of illness: ____

- Duration of illness: ______________________

- Cause of illness according to participants.________________________

- Type of treatment taken before reporting to Yoga Centre:________________

- Benefits/adverse effect of previous treatment________________________________

- Willingness for admission to hospital/out patient__________________________________

PRESENT COMPLAINTS (If any): Physical:

- Fever
- Pain
- Swelling of particular region
- Defect in vision, hearing, smell, taste, touch and headache
- Complaints regarding digestive system :
- Less of appetite,
- Indigestion
- Diarrhea
- Constipation
- Feeling of tiredness/lack of energy

Complaints regarding movements of limbs: Inability to work with hand. Swelling of various joints

- Complaints regarding spine: Pain in neck, Backache
- Respiratory Circulatory System:
- Breathlessness: Without exertion
    - With slight exertion
    - Cough
    - Palpitation
    - Swelling over feet
    - Complaints suggestion of affection of mind
    - Lack of desire to work
    - Lack of decision making.
    - Disturbance in adjustment with family members, friends
    - Lack of adjustment with working condition/work

EXAMINATION OF PATICIPANTS:

- Status of general health assessment: Good / Average / Poor
- Expression on face:
- Expression in eyes:
- Height: ________CMS.
- Weight: _________ kg.
- Inspection of limbs/spine
- Pulse: ________B.P.: ______/_______ Resp.Rate: ________
- Examination of
    - Nose:
    - Mouth:
    - Teeth:
    - Skin:

Signature of Medical officer
With comments

Camp Report:

To
The Secretary, /HOD.,
Kaivalyadhām. / *UGC/ Ayush/ MHRD*
Lonavla: 410 403.

Sub.: Yoga Camp Report held at: NDL
Dear Sir,

As per the instruction, I submit herewith the report[1] of the above camp. The camp ended on _____________. We returned from camp duty on ___________ and joined the department on______________ at ______am/pm

NAME OF THE ORGANISATION GROUP/PUBLIC	CAMP ORGANSED (IN DAYS)	NO. OF PARTICIPANTS MALE	FEMALE	TOTAL NO.

Morning Class
Practices taught

Day/After noon theory
Subjects taught

Evening Class
Practices taught

Thanking you,
Yours faithfully,

(SKG)
Camp In-charge

APPENDICES

Appendix - I

A Comparative Study of Four Yoga Practices:

UDDIYANA, AGNISARA, KAPALBHATI AND NAULI

INTRODUCTION:

Uddiyana, Agnisara, Kapalabhati and Nauli are very efficacious and very important among the practices constituting the Yogic system of physical education. While differing from one another these practices have some points of similarity. It is, therefore, proposed to bring out clearly some salient points of comparison between these practices so that every practice could be clearly understood and not mixed up with other practices and cause a confusion in the practitioner's mind. At the same time we learn the technique of a particular practice better by nothing the points of difference between seemingly the same practices. Keeping this in view the following details have been worked out for the benefit of the practical students of Yoga.

POINTS COMMON TO ALL THE FOUR PRACTICES :

1. All of them are capable of being practised in the sitting position, though, except Kapalabhati, all could be advantageously practised in "standing with bent shoulder" position.
2. All these practices have an exhalatory retention phase except, Kapalabhati.
3. All these practices involve play of abdominal muscles.
4. All of these promote peristaltic movement.

INTER-COMPARISON OF THE FOUR PRACTICES :

UDDIYANA AND AGNISARA:

Common points :

Both are performed after complete exhalation which is maintained throughout the exercise.

Points of Difference :

1. In Uddiyana the main action is Mock inhalation. In Agnisara this is to be scrupulously avoided.
2. In Uddiyana abdominal muscles are kept relaxed while in Agnisara abdominal muscles are kept contracted.
3. Uddiyana gives a concave appearance to the abdominen. There is no such concavity seen in Agnisara.
4. In Agnisara the abdominal region near the navel (lower abdomen) takes a part, while in Uddiyana the abdomen above and below the navel comes into play.
5. The position once taken up in Uddiyana is to be maintained throughout. Agnisara consists in an alternate movement of vigorous contraction and protrusion of the abdomen.
6. Uddiyana is an exercise mainly of thoracic diaphragm while Agnisara is that of pelvic diaphragm.

UDDIYANA AND KAPALABHATI:

Common points :

Uddiyana and Kapalbhati are both diaphragmatic exercises.

Points of Difference :

1. Uddiyana is stationary while in Kapalabhati movement of the abdominal muscles takes place with every inhalation and exhalation.
2. Uddiyana can be done either sitting or standing. But Kapalabhati is invariably done in the sitting position, preferably in Padmasana.
3. In Kapalabhati chest is fixed in a little elevated position and the action is performed by the abdominal muscles. In Uddiyana abdominal muscles play a passive role, the active role being played by thorax. The process of mock-inhalation consists Sin expansion of chest without allowing the air to get in.
4. The efficiency of the practice of Kapalabhati is judged by the speed and the thythm of inhalation and exhalation. On the other hand, efficiency of Uddiyana lies in maintenance of the position for a prolonged period after the correct position is take up.

UDDIYANA AND NAULI:

Common Points :

1. Both can be practised in sitting, or better, in standing position.
2. Both are done under the exhalatory retention condition.
3. In both negative pressure is created in the internal cavities and is used for sucking liquids in the body cavities.

Points of Difference :

1. Uddiyana forms a preliminary practice for Nauli. The way of Nauli lies through Uddiyana. Nauli is further development of Uddiyana. We can say Nauli = Uddiyana + Isolation and rolling manipulation of the abdominal recti. In Nauli greater amount of negative pressure is produced in the internal cavities.

AGNISARA AND KAPALBHATI :

Common Points :

1. Both are abdominal exercises of a repetitive nature. But in Agnisara the action is repeated slowly, while in Kapalabhati it is done with speed which is ideally fixed at 120 repetitions per minute.
2. The region of contraction of the abdomen is around the navel in both exercises.

Points of Difference :

1. In Agnisara the abdominal muscles (especially of the lower abdomen) are moved back and forth after complete exhalation in Kapalabhati the exhalation is done by inward strokes of the lower abdomen and inhalation automatic as the abdominal wall comes to its normal position.
2. Agnisara deals with pelvic diaphragm while Kapalabhati works mainly on the thoracic diaphragm.

AGNISARA AND NAULI:

Common points:

1. Both are practised under exhalation.
2. Both deal with the abdominal muscles.

Points of Difference:

1. In Agnisara there is an attempt at mock exhalation*, for contraction. Such a contraction comes in the way of isolation of recti in Nauli. The second part of Agnisara containing protrusion has some similarity with the attempt at isolatiionof recti in Nauli. But for satisfactory isolation of recti in Nauli, the essential feature is that of mock inhalation and not of mock exhalation.
2. Kapalabhati is a type of breathing exercise including speedy and incessant inhalations and exhalations, maintaining a fixed rhythm. Nauli may also be called a breathing exercise but of a different nature. Inhalations and exhalations form the essential feature of Kapalabhati. Nauli, as a breathing exercise, differs from Kapalabhati in that it is retention of breath outside (which is termed Bahya Kumbhaka).
3. In Kapalabhati abdominal muscles are alternately contracted and relaxed as a whole; while in Nauli the abdominal recti are isolated from the other abdominal Muscles, their vigorous contraction is maintained and they are differentiated and alternatively contracted and relaxed to give the appearance of the wave.

SUMMARY:

The four Yogic practices, namely, Uddiyana, Agnisara, Kapalabhati and Nauli are very efficacious and important. While differing from one another, these practices have some points of similarity. When learning the technique of a particular practice we learn better and quicker by noting the points of difference between seemingly the same practices. It was, therefore, thought necessary to present in this intercomparisons of these four practices for the benefit of the practical students.

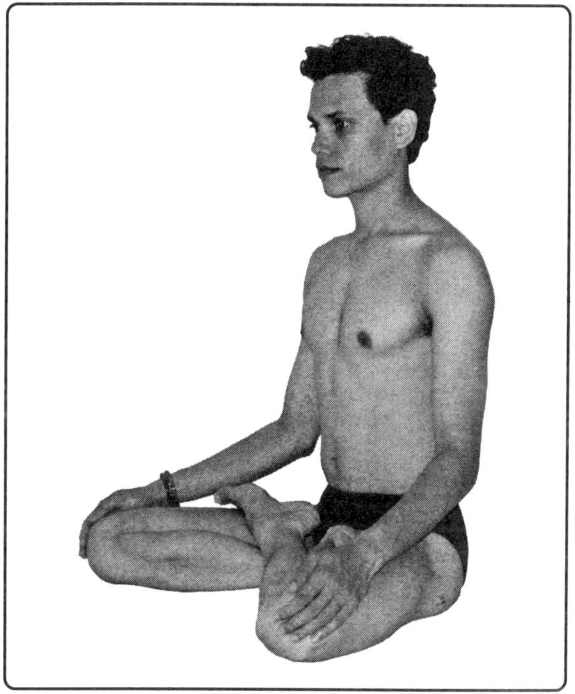

KAPALABHATI
Inward stroke of abdomen at navel region with sudden exhalation

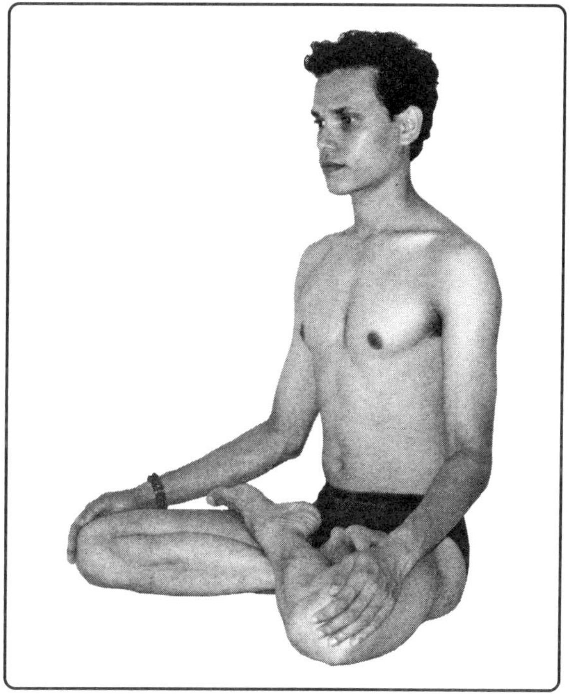

KAPALABHATI
Relaxation of the abdomen to be accompanied by inhalation

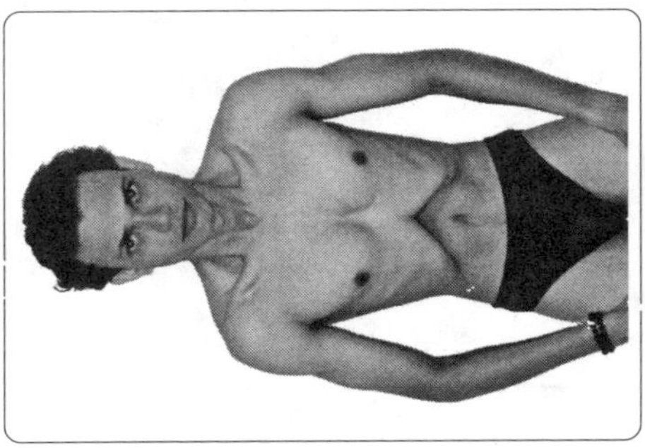

UDDIYANA

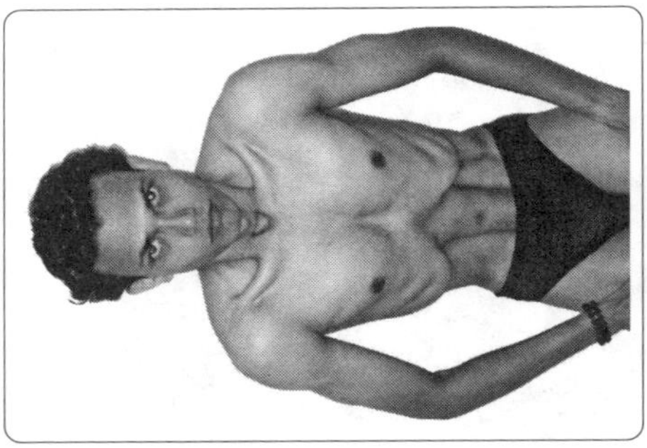

NAULI
(Madhyama)

AGNISARA
Vigorous retraction of the lower abdomen

AGNISARA
Vigorous protrusion of the lower abdomen

Appendix - II

SALIENT POINTS OF THE YOGIC PRACTICES

There are certain important points that contribute to the efficient learning and performance of the Yogic practices. These should be known by the students so that they derive pleasure and satisfaction from the performance of these practices. These vital points are useful in some practices not only in avoiding discomfort but also to prevent possible injuries. With this in view the salient points of the selected Yogic practices have been described here. It is taken for granted that the readers are acquainted with the technique of the practices mentioned in this article.

Shirshasana

It should not be practised immediately after any violent exercise. 2) The centre of the head should be placed on the ground to rest the whole body vertically. 3) Throwing up the legs with jerk should be carefully avoided. 4) Proceed from one stage to another after having mastered the former stages in order to get confidence to do the practice without anybody's help. *Limitations:* Should be avoided in case of aching or running ears, weak eye capillaries, high blood pressure, heart troubles, etc.

Progression : 1) Ardha Halasana
2) Halasana,
3) Viparita Karani
4) Sarvangasana
5) Shirshasana.

Sarvangasana

Raise the legs very slowly till they stand vertically resting on shoulders. 2) Press the trunk with hands against the chin till it is well set in the jugular notch.

Progression : 1) Ardha Halasana 2) Viparita Karani,
3) Sarvangasana

Matsyasana

Try to take the maximum arch of the spine. 2) Foot lock should be raised up while arching the back. 3) It should be practised as a complementary pose to "Sarvangasana" to reap good advantages.

Progression: 1) Padmasana
2) Supta Vajrasana
3) Matsyasana

Halasana

People having stiff spine should practise this very slowly. Whatever little bent is possible should first be secured and maintained for some time. 2) Raise the legs slowly avoiding jerky movements.

Progression: 1) Ardha Halasana 2) Viparitakarani

Bhujangasana

The trunk is to be raised only upto the navel and not beyond it. 2) Least pressure should be exerted on the hands. 3) Hands are to be bent in elbow and not to be kept straight. Distance between the elbows should be minimum. 4) A wave of contraction and relaxation travelling up and down the spinal column is the principal feature of this pose.

Ardha Shalabhasana

A leg should be raised to the point where the pelvis dose not tilt sidewards. 2) Knees are to be kept straight.

Shalabhasana

Knees are kept together and straight while raising the legs. 2) Raising of the legs should be smooth avoiding any jerk. 3) Close fists keeping knuckles down to get good support in raising the legs.

Progression: 1) Ardha Shalabhasana
2) Shalabhasana

Dhanurasana

In case of beginners the knees may be kept apart. Later on they should be drawn closer, and at last they should be made to stand together. 2) Secure greater curve of the body in order to bring about maximum pressure on the abdominal region. 3) Hands are to be kept straight. 4) Look up as much as possible.

Progression: 1) Bhujangasana 2) Ardha Shalabhasana 3) Shalabhasana 4) Dhanurasana

Vakrasana

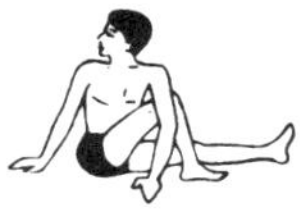

The foot of the bent leg is to be placed by the side of the knee of extended leg. 2) The hand placed at the back should be at such a distance as would keep the trunk erect. 3) Press the raised knee with upper arm.

Ardha-Matsyendrasana

The main feature of the pose consists in twisting the spinal column. 2) The erect knee acts as a fulcrum for getting a maximum twist. 3) Heel is to be kept right against the perineum. One should not sit on the heel. 4) Bring the armpit closer to the raised knee to get better twist. 5) Trunk should be kept erect. 6) Look as far back as possible.

Progression : 1) Vakrasana 2) Chakrasana 3) Ardha Matsyendrasana.

Paschimatana

Knee should be kept stiff. 2) Avoid all sorts of jerks either mild of violent. 3) The trunk should be bent forward comfortably and maintained as long as possible without much discomfort. The maintenance will invariably make further flexion possible. 4) Grasping of toes should not be emphasised in the initial stage of practice.

Progression: 1) Padhastasana 2) Halasana 3) Paschimatana

Vajrasana

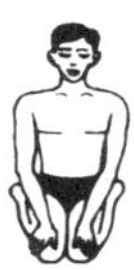

Do not sit on heels. 2) Keep the trunk erect. 3) Draw the knees closer.

Supta-Vajrasana

Do not rest on heels. Adjust your feet so as to rest the pelvis between them or keep the heels out. 2) To lie on the back go slowly with the support of hands. 3) Take special care of ankle joints. 4) Keep the knees together. Beginners may initially keep them apart.

Progression : 1) Vajrasana 2) Supta Vajrasana

Utkatasana

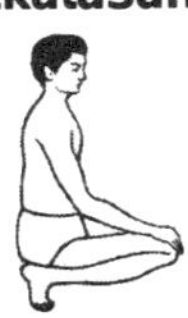

The heels should be raised to the extent of making an angle of about 45 degrees to the ground. 2) Keep the trunk erect. 3) The thighs should be parallel and as far as possible horizontal to the ground.

Bakasana

Spread your fingers pointing them forward and take good support. 2) Keep the elbows straight. Care should be taken that while raising the foot-lock no pressure is exerted on the elbow joints.
Progression: 1) Padmasana 2) Lolasana 3) Bakasana

Tolangulasana

Balance on your fists. 2) Lift the buttocks. 3) Raise the foot-lock and the trunk from both sides making an angle of about 30 degrees to the ground.
Progression : 1) Ardha Padmasana 2) Padmasana 3) Tolangulasana

Kukkutasana

Spread the fingers well to take firm support. Fingers should point forward. 2) Try to keep the trunk erect. 3) Look front 4) Insert your hands as much as you can through the space near the ankles.
Progression : 1) Padmasana 2) Kukkutasana-bandha (Inserting hands.)

Mayurasana

Fingers should be well spread out in order to secure broad base. 2) Keep the elbow together and place them near the navel. 3) The forearms should incline forward and not stand exactly at right angles to the ground. 4) Propel your body forward till the feet are lifted up.
Progression: 1) Hamsasana 2) Mayurasana

Chakrasana

Keep the feet together avoiding any angle. 2) Keep the raised hand close to the ear. 3) Do not bend at the elbow . 4) Do not bend at the loins.

Vrikshasana

The knee of the folded leg should project sideward. 2) Any bend in the loins should be avoided.

Agnisara

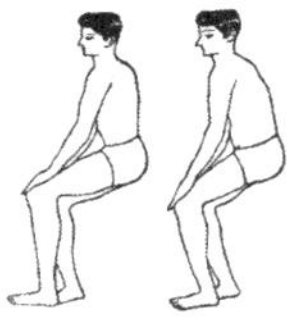

Deepest possible exhalation should be accompanied by general contraction of the navel region. 2) Further vigorous contraction. 3) Avoid slightest inhalatory effort that may cause raising of the ribs (otherwise one will go to Uddiyana). 4) Abdomen should be stiff enough in both retraction and in protrusion.

Uddiyana

Assume bent position of the trunk. 2) Deepest possible exhalation followed by vigorous mock inhalation. 3) Relax the front abdominal muscles.

Progression: 1) Preliminary practice in chest raising with and without inhalation. 2) (Mock inhalation) Uddiyana.

Nauli

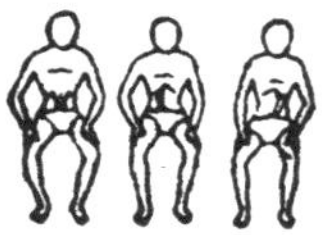

Limitations: Should be practised with an empty stomach. Should be avoided in case of any abdominal pain, high blood pressure and boys and girls before the age of puberty. Maintain Uddiyana and relax abdominal muscles. 2) Bend the trunk, flex the knees and elbows and maintain the round back position throughout the practice. 3) Avoid movements of the buttocks, if there be any. 4) Avoid straining action. *Nauli Chalan :*

Clockwise: Uddiyana- Vama Nauli-Madnya Nauli-Dakshina Nauli-Uddiyana.

Anti-Clockwise : Uddiyana-Dakshina Nauli-Madhya Nauli-Vama Nauli-Uddiyana.

Progression : 1) Uddiyana 2) Relax abdominal Muscles in Uddiyana 3) Madhya Nauli 4) Vama and Dakshina Nauli from Madhya Nauli 5) Vama and Dakshina Nauli from Uddiyana.

Kapalabhati

Exhale suddenly and forcibly giving an abdominal stroke inward at the navel region. 2) Relax the abdomen fully and inhale. Thus inhalation should be passive and as a result of relaxation of abdominal muscles. 3) No contortions on face. 4) Chest should be fixed up in order to have least movement of it 5) Speed should not be increased at the cost of efficiency.

Progression : 1) Preliminary practice in voluntary Contraction and relaxation of the abdomen.

2) Practice of voluntary Contraction of lower abdomen with exhalation and relaxation of abdomen with passive inhalation. 3) Adjust proper speed and rhythm.

Ujjayi

Inhale through nose with frictional sound produced from partial contraction of the glottis. 2) Expand the chest and control the abdomen so that it does not bulge out too much. 3) Very slowly exhale heaving down the chest gradually and then retract the abdomen. 4) Inhalation should not be hurried up as a result of slow exhalation.

Shavasana

Take best body position offering least resistance to the gravity. 2) Keep the body immobile. 3) A little deeper diaphragmatic breathing. 4) Eyes closed. 5) Attend to the flow of breath at the nose.

Makrasana

Take prone lying position by keeping both the legs apart and toes pointing untoward and heels besting or the ground. Place both the hands or opposite shoulders and head in between both the arms, Eyes closed. Resort to the little deeper breathing.

Appendix - III

Model Question Paper

Q.1. What are those principles that a Yoga Teacher also should keep in mind? Give Examples.

Q.2. How do you define "Class Management"? What are those points to be kept in mind for a good Class Management?

Q.3. What are the principles of Pranayama?

Q.4. What are the principles and basic steps of selecting teaching aids? What are the advantages of teaching aids?

Q.5. Name the methods used in Teaching with examples.

Q.6. What are the steps of an ideal lesson plan? Prepare one lesson plan on any "Balancing Asana" for 20 minutes duration.

Q.7. What are those salient points to be remembered and advantages of the following yogic practices?

1. Ujjayi, 2. Yoga Mudra

Model Question Paper

Q.1. Define "Method". What are the advantages of Method?

Q.2. What are the principles of Pranayama?

Q.3. What are the advantages of Teaching aids?

Q.4. What are the differences between Asana and Exercise?

Q.5. How do you define class management? What are those points to be kept in mind for a good class management?

Q.6. What are the those kinds of Questions? Discuss with example.

Q.7. What are those salient points and advantages of the following yogic practices?

1. Bhujangasana, 2. Yoga Mudra

SHIRSHASANA

VIPRITKARNI

SARVANGASANA

MATSYASANA

HALASANA

1

2

3

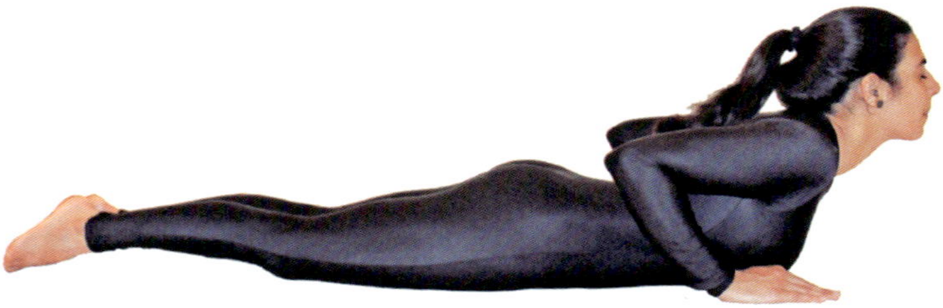

4

BHUJANGASANA

1

2

3

4

5

ARDHA-SHALBHASANA

1

2

3

SHALBHASANA

1

2

3

4

5

DHANURASANA

VAKRASANA

1

2

3

4

5

6

ARDHA-MATSYENDRASANA

PASCHIMATANA

VAJRASANA

SUPTA-VAJRASANA

YOGAMUDRA

UTKATASANA

BAKASANA

TOLANGULASANA

KUKUTASANA

MAYURASANA

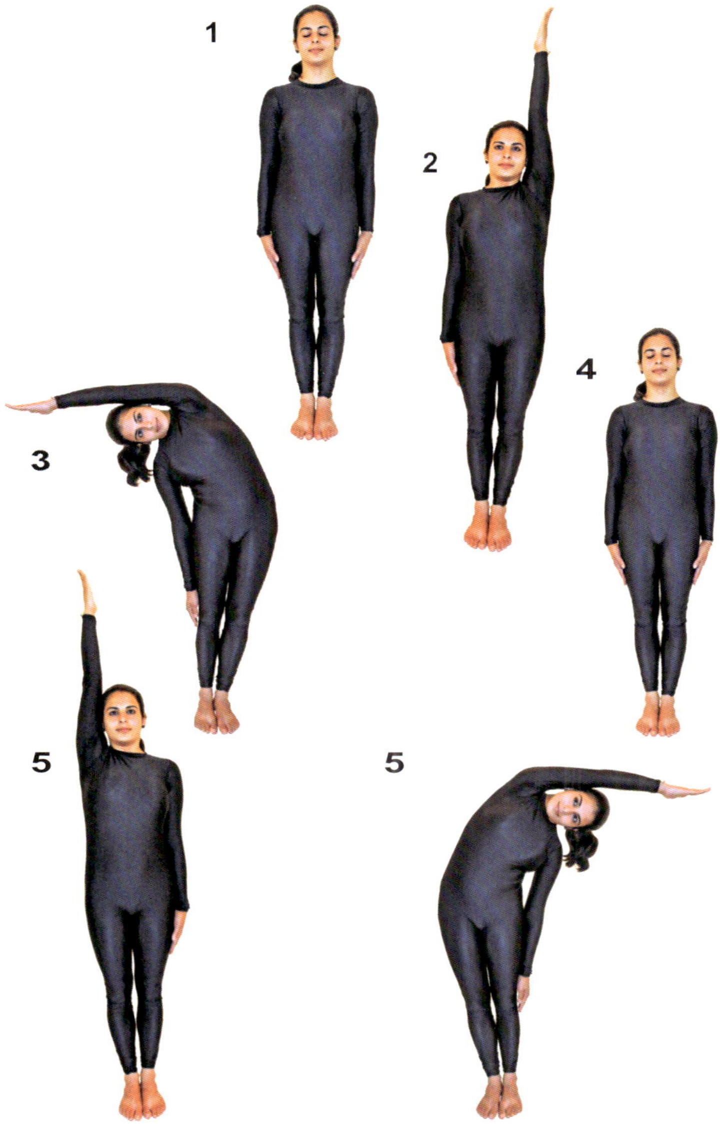

CHAKRASANA

1

2

3

4

5

6

VRIKSHASANA

1

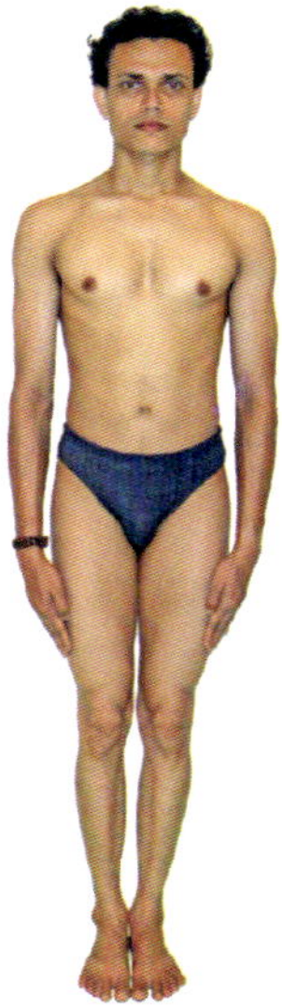

2

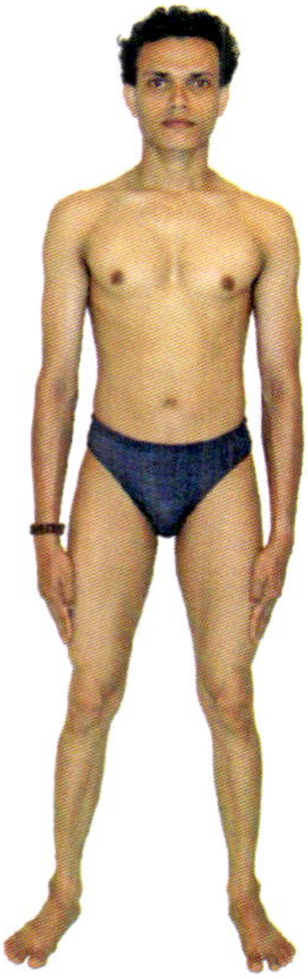

3

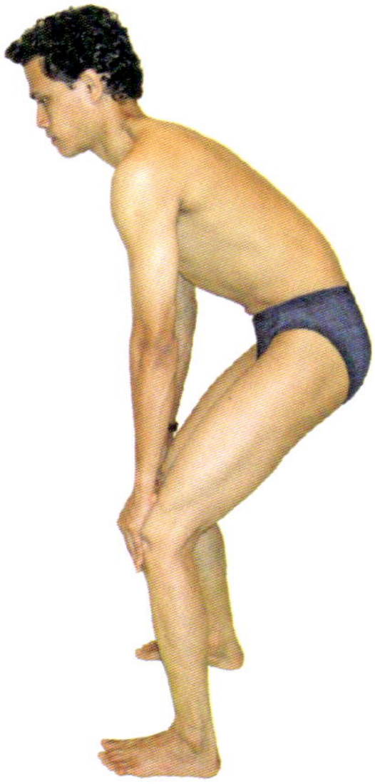

4

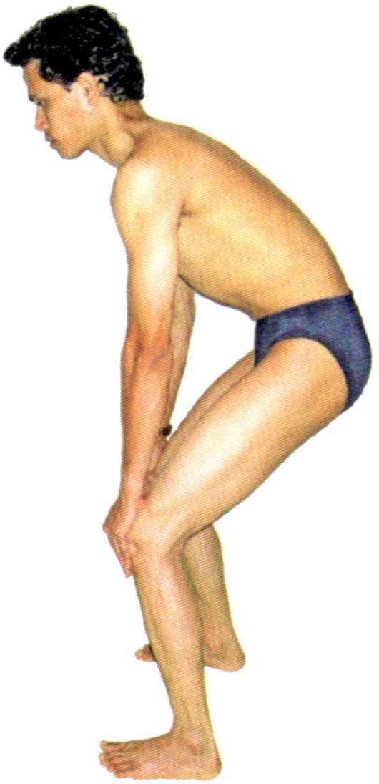

AGNISARA

1

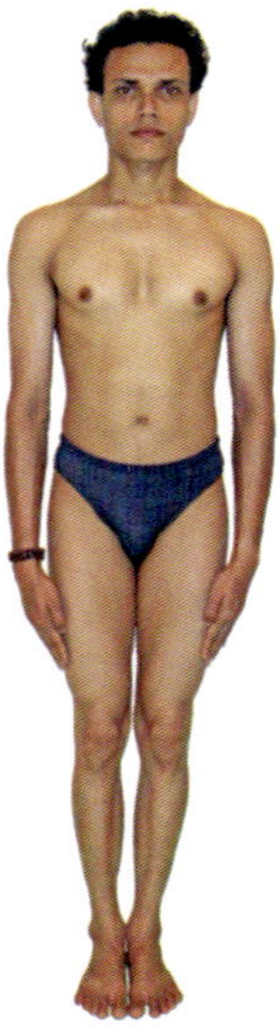

2

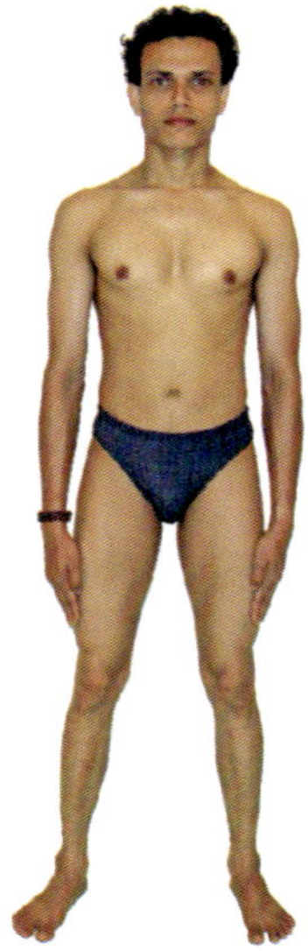

3

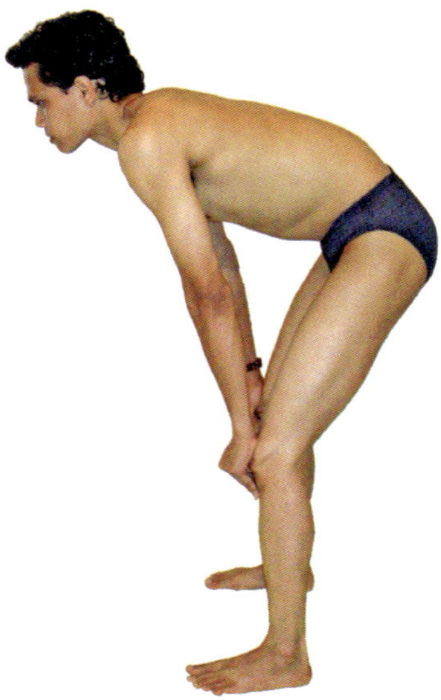

4

UDDIYANABANDHA

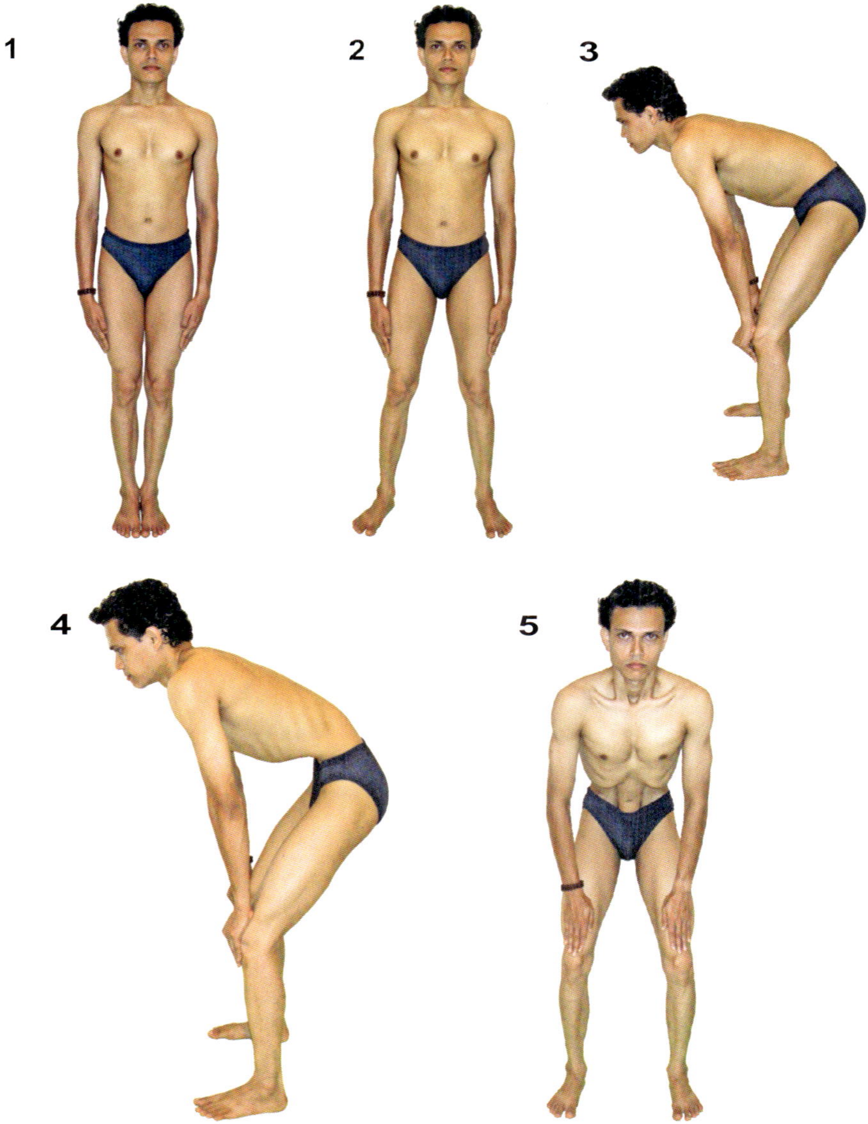

MADHAYA NAULI

KAPALABHATI

1

2

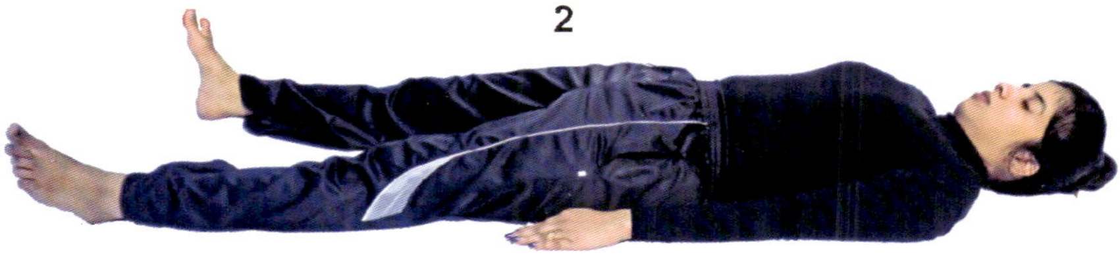

3

SHAVASANA

YOGIC PRACTICES

SHIRSHASANA

VIPRITKARNI

SARVANGASANA

MATSYASANA

HALASANA

BHUJANGASANA

ARDHA-SHALBHASANA

SHALBHASANA

DHANURASANA

VAKRASANA

ARDHA MATSYENDRASANA

PASCHIMATANA

VAJRASANA

SUPTA-VAJRASANA

YOGAMUDRA

UTKATASANA

BAKASANA

TOLANGULASANA

KUKUTASANA

MAYURASANA

CHAKRASANA

VRIKSHASANA

AGNISARA

UDDIYANABANDHA

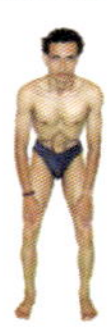
MADHAYA NAULI

KAPALABHATI

SHAVASANA

INDEX

INDEX

FURTHER READING

BOOKS

1. C. Knapp and E. Patricia Hagman. **Teaching Methods for Physical Education,** McGraw-Hill Book Company, Inc. 1953.
2. Donald G. Butler, **Teaching Yoga,** Geoffrey Chapman Publishers, 1975.
3. K.K Bhatia and J .N. Arora, **Methodology of Teaching,** Prakash Brothers, Ludhiana, 1985.
4. M.L. Gharote, **Guidelines for Yogic Practices,** Medha Publications, Lonavla, 1982.
5. M.L. Kamalesh, and Sangral, M.S. **METHODS IN PHYSICAL EDUCATION**, Ludhiana: Parkash Brothers Educational Publishers, pp.39-45, 1985.
6. Ruth L. Murray and Della P. Hussey, **From Student to Teacher in Physical Education,** Prentice-Hall, Inc. 1959.
7. Swami Kuvalayananda, **Asanas,** Kaivalyadhama, Lonavla, 1983.
8. Swami Kuvalayananda, **Pranayama,** Kaivalyadhama, Lonavla, 1983.
9. Swami Kuvalayananda, S.L. Vinekar, **Yogic Therapy**, DGHS, Ministry of Health, Govt. of India, 1963.
10. S.K. Kochhar, **METHODS AND TECHNIQUES OF TEACHING,** New Delhi: Sterling Publishers Private Limited, pp.134-187, 1990.
11. Swami. Ramsukhadas, **Srimad Bhâgvad Gitâ**, (Vol.I-Second edition.) Gorakhpur: Gitapress, pp. 562, 2001.
12. **Sachitra Shaley Yogabhyaskram,** (Marathi) Director, Sports and Youth Welfare, Pune 1976.
13. Tiwari, O.P. and G.S.Sahay, **Asânâs-Why and How ?,** Kaivalyadhama: Lonavla, 1984.
14. **Yogâsanâs a Teacher's Guide,** Written by Prof. S.K.Ganguly, New Delhi: NCERT, 1983.

ARTICLES

1. M.L. Gharote, "Group Technique of Introducing Yogic Practices", **Yoga-Mimāmsā,** 13:4: 41-44, Jan. 1971.

2. M.V. Bhole, "Lesson Plan for Introducing the Concept of Pranayama Breathing in a class of Beginners", **Yoga-Mimāmsā,** 20: 1 & 2: 44-49, 1979.

3. M.V. Bhole, S.K. Ganguly, "Lesson Plan to introduce the Concept of Āsanas in a Class of Beginners", **Vyāyām-Vidnyān,** Amravati, 14:4: 1- 4, 1981.

4. S.K. Ganguly, "Teaching Yogasana Lesson", **Yoga-Mimāmsā,** 19: 2 & 3: 75-84, 1977-78.

5. S.K. Ganguly and A.M. Moorthy, "Selected Points on Method of Yoga Practice Teaching", **Yoga-Mimāmsā,** Vol. XVIII - 2, pp. 29-35, 1976.

6. S.K.Ganguly, "Art and Science of Questioning in Yoga Teaching", **Yoga-Mimāmsā** Lonavla:Kaivalyadhama,35:3 & 4:255-262, 2003.

7. **S.K.**Ganguly, (1983). The 14th Yoga Camp held at New Delhi: A report. *Yoga-Mimāmsā*, Lonavla: Kaivalyadhām, *21*, 3&4,104-106.

8. S.K.Gangly,(1998). Yogic Researches in Kaivalyadhām-An overview, *Souvenir*, Kaivalyadhām: Mumbai: I.C.Y. Health Centre, pp.59-68.